The Complete
MEXICAN
COOKBOOK

The Complete
MEXICAN
·COOKBOOK·

LOURDES NICHOLS

PIATKUS

First published in 1995 by
Judy Piatkus (Publishers) Ltd
5 Windmill Street, London W1P 1HF

The moral right of the author has been asserted
A catalogue record for this book is available from the British Library

ISBN 0-7499-1550-1

Designed by Paul Saunders
Photographs by Gus Filgate
Food for photography prepared by Louise Pickford
Photographic styling by Penny Markham

Cover photograph by Martin Brigdale shows Guacamole (page 48),
Totopos (page 46), Piccadillo (page 139), Arroz Blanco (page 98)
and Rajas de Chile Poblano (page 170)

Typeset by Computerset Ltd, Harmondsworth
Printed and bound in Great Britain by
Bath Press PLC, Bath, Avon

CONTENTS

▲▲▲▲▲▲▲▲▲▲▲▲▲▲▲▲

INTRODUCTION

Like a true Mexican, and like so many people who live away from the place in which they grew up, I miss my country, my family and my friends, and I miss the familiar smells of the flowers, the markets and those glorious cooking aromas prevalent in my home. My marriage took me away from Mexico and, since then, I have tried to bring the flavours of Mexico to me. I feel well rewarded and deeply grateful, both to my native country for providing me with its richness, and to England, my adopted country, for being so responsive to my efforts.

When I first came to England, in 1967, it was virtually impossible to cook Mexican food due to the lack of ingredients. My longing for authentic Mexican food started me on a search for basic ingredients which culminated in my efforts to make it available to the people of Europe and to fellow Mexicans here who, like me, were longing to eat the real thing. While some of the ingredients might seem difficult to find, once you know where to look your task is simple. Large supermarkets have introduced a myriad of ethnic products, many of which can be adapted to Mexican cooking. Indian, Chinese and West Indian shops all contribute to the Mexican pantry, aided by Italian, Spanish and Greek delicatessens.

I am delighted to say that the storekeepers of Britain and Europe are ever more ready to stock exotic ingredients which, only five years ago, were unheard of. Thus, it is now possible to find fresh corn and flour *tortillas* in larger supermarkets and speciality shops, *chorizo* at delicatessens and ready-salted *tortilla* chips in many of the multiples.

With the support of my husband and children, my mother's encouragement, the interest of my American friends who wanted to learn to cook Mexican food, and the assistance of my Mexican friends in sending me the ingredients I could not find in Britain, I finally managed to obtain all I required to enable me to teach Mexican cooking and to sell my own home-made products.

Word of my lessons and sales of home-made Mexican food soon got around and it was not long before I was giving courses in Mexican cooking and writing books. Slowly I built up a business which I ran from home whilst looking after my business-executive husband, my ageing mother and my three children. The food and the books created their own demand and within a few years I found myself producing Mexican food in such large quantities that commercial premises were essential if I were to continue. So an idea that started with a two-kilogram bag of *masa* (maize flour) has developed into a fully fledged business importing over 500 tons of *masa* a year, selling *tortillas* (unleavened pancakes), *tortilla* chips and all manner of other Mexican delicacies to the catering trade and main supermarkets in the British Isles as well as exporting to most European countries.

Mexico City is a cosmopolitan gourmet centre which has adopted popular international dishes to suit its own tastes and needs. The great variety of ingredients available there, combined with the flair and ingenuity of its cooks, has earned Mexico a well-deserved place in the world of cookery. Mexican cuisine is varied and tasty, featuring dishes with colour, texture and interest.

I am increasingly faced with a demand for the kind of specialised information that only a book of this scale can satisfy. I can't help but feel that those people who have found pleasure in my previous books on Mexican food will have developed a desire to delve deeper into the mysteries and adventures to which they have become exposed. Sometimes I find it hard to believe the lengths to which some people will go in order to track me down to my Buckinghamshire *tortillería* (*tortilla* factory) just to ask for advice on the preparation of an unusual dish or to enquire whether we sell a particular ingredient.

I have chosen to include in this volume the better-known Mexican dishes which have strongly contributed to Mexico's good gourmet name. In many cases it has been necessary to use substitute ingredients in order to prepare a traditional dish. My hope is that, eventually, authentic canned Mexican products will also be readily available in this country.

An appreciation of the cuisine of any country is greatly enhanced by an understanding of the geographical and historical background that led to its development. The following brief outline of Mexico's geography and history will, I hope, assist in your understanding of its culture and give you the confidence to cook a Mexican meal using your own imagination and according to your own tastes.

THE LIE OF THE LAND

Geographically, Mexico lies to the south of the United States of (North) America, with whom it shares a natural boundary – the Rio Bravo, also known as the Rio Grande. The bordering American states are California, Arizona, New Mexico and Texas. To the south, Mexico borders with the Central American states of Gautemala and Belize, to the west and south-west lies the Pacific Ocean, and to the east the Gulf of Mexico and the Caribbean Sea. It also has two large peninsulas – Yucatán in the south-east and Baja California with its Golfo de Cortés in the north-west.

Its geographical location on both sides of the Tropic of Cancer and its wide range of elevation, with the Sierra Madre cutting through the length of the country until it becomes the Rocky Mountains in North America, provide Mexico with varied climatic conditions, from tropical rain-forests to deserts and snow-capped volcanoes. The land along the 10,000 kilometres of coast is tropical, supplying the country not only with a wide variety of fish and shellfish, but also with citrus and tropical fruits such as coconuts, sweet and sour sop, sugar-cane, paw-paw, avocados, mangoes and a wide variety of bananas and other fruits and vegetables native to Mexico which have not yet made their international debut, like the fruits of the 'zapodilla' family.

A different range of crops, such as maize, beans, chillies and vegetables, are cultivated on the mountain slopes and higher plateaux where the heat is tempered by the altitude. Upon reaching the highest inhabited points, where the climate is cooler, coffee and cereals, such as wheat, oats and barley, are grown. Above lie the snow-capped volcanoes which dot the Mexican landscape like an offering in the bright blue sky. The lava or volcanic rock from the volcanic eruptions features in some native cookery implements, like the *molcajete and tejolote* (mortar and pestle), *metate* (three-legged stone grinder) and *mexalpilli* (rolling pin).

Due to its varied climate – that of *Tierra Caliente* (tropical zone), *Tierra Templada* (semi-tropical zone) and *Tierra Fria* (cold zone) – Mexico exhibits a remarkable variety of flora and fauna. The flora includes valuable woods, medicinal plants and mushrooms, and an extensive variety of fruits and vegetables as well as very many wild and cultivated flowers. Its fauna comprises many types of fish from the seas, rivers, lakes and mountain streams as well as birds of brilliant plumage varying in size from the tiny *chupamirto* (humming-bird) to the large *uexólotl* (turkey).

Mexico also has vast areas of desert and arid land which are suitable for growing cactuses and agaves. The *nopal* is widely eaten raw or cooked as a vegetable and the various types of agaves provide the country with a variety of drinks like tequila and mezcal.

Agriculture

It is estimated that man first arrived in the Americas around 35,000 years ago, that he was nomadic and that he depended on hunting and fishing for his existence. There is some controversy as to where he originated, but the theory that he came in small family groups through the Bering Strait seems the most probable. There does not appear to be any exact data as to the beginning of agriculture in the Americas, but Mexico is considered to be one of the first places in that continent where man started to cultivate edible plants like maize and beans, and to domesticate animals like the turkey.

The main diet consisted of *cinteotl* (maize), used for making *tlaxcalli* (tortillas), which provided carbohydrates, calcium and vitamin B; beans, rich in fibre, gave the Mexicans most of their daily protein requirements; chillies, the third most important crop for the Mexican peasant, provided valuable vitamin C when consumed fresh, and vitamin A when prepared dried. Wild animals, turkey, duck, pigeon, pheasant, dog, wild pig, and a large variety of fish were eaten regularly; iguana and snake were eaten occasionally. Courgettes featured heavily in the Mexican's diet, not only because they were tasty and added variety, but when planted together with the maize plant, *milpa*, its large leaves provided welcome shade to the roots and assisted in keeping the earth moist.

Maize, beans, tomatoes, the green-husked tomatillos, avocados, cactus, pumpkins, chillies of assorted colours and sizes, paw-paw, pineapples, peanuts, cacao, and vanilla are among the products Mexico has offered to the world. Other native crops are cotton, tobacco, sisal and rubber. Potatoes are believed to have come from Peru along the Pacific coast on board Spanish galleons when they stopped in Mexico for cargo.

Although the land is good and there are vast amounts of it, Mexico's agricultural resources are under-exploited due to lack of irrigation. As a result, the staple foods, maize, beans and chillies, are dried and consumed during the winter months, calling for different cooking methods.

After the discovery of America by Christopher Columbus in 1492 and the Spanish conquest of Mexico by Hernán Cortés in 1520, sugar-cane, olive oil, wine, wheat, chickens, pigs, hooved animals, citrus fruits, rice, onions, garlic and spices were introduced to the New World and acclimatised easily. In this way, the native diet of Mexico was enriched in nutritional value and variety. Naturally, new methods of cooking had to be adopted to integrate these new ingredients into the native cooking methods and Mexicans today enjoy a healthy, nutritious and most exciting cuisine.

With the arrival of the Spaniards, agriculture took a big leap forward and the use of animal manure and tilling methods with oxen were soon to reap big rewards.

A CHEQUERED HISTORY

Native Mexican Indians

The early history of Mexico is obscure and based on legend rather than fact, but it appears that Anahuac (the Lake Country), now Mexico City, was first populated by the noble, talented and religious Nahua people called Toltecs who can be traced back to the seventh century. To them are ascribed the arts and religions and the pyramids of Teotihuacán. In the fourteenth century came the Chichimecas who were excellent tradesmen and handicraft people. They were finally taken over by the Aztecs, warriors and cultured people whose civilisation flourished. They founded a powerful empire in the Valley of Mexico some three or four hundred years before the discovery of America.

Their food was simple but very healthy, mostly boiled or steamed with hand-patted corn *tortillas* to accompany every meal. The markets were well attended and trading was done by barter. Cacao (cocoa) beans were used instead of money when necessary; gold and silver had little value other than their ornamental beauty. Moctezuma, the Aztec Emperor, lived in a palace with beautiful gardens, fountains, flowers and animals. He is said to have had 1,000 freshly cooked dishes to choose from at every meal. As a routine, his food was tasted by his courtesans in order to prevent him being poisoned.

Fresh fish from the coast brought by relays of barefooted runners were delivered at his palace daily. He drank *xoco-latli* (chocolate), a bitter-sweet drink, and wore capes of brilliant colours which had feathers sewn in intricate patterns. His treasure consisted of granaries full of cocoa beans rather than gold and silver. These eventually cost him his life as the Spaniards would not accept that he was not hiding from them the gold and silver they so valued, and tortured him to death hoping to find out where the non-existent gold was.

The Aztecs were the most aggressive and prosperous tribe in Mexico at the time of the discovery of America. They provoked wars with neighbouring tribes who had to pay them tribute in the shape of cocoa beans, corn, beans and prisoners for human sacrifices.

The Spanish Conquest

The defeat of the Aztec Empire by Hernán Cortés and a handful of Spanish adventurers is one of the most startling military feats in history. Cortés tricked the Indians into submission and burnt his boats so his men could not desert him.

The first Spanish city on Mexican territory was called Villa Rica de la Vera Cruz (rich valley of the true cross). Rich it was indeed, with more than a surplus of fowl, wild pigs, fish, fruits and vegetables as well as an abundance of wild and beautiful flowers and orchids. (The pods of an orchid found in these lands have given us vanilla which was used by the natives to flavour their drinking chocolate.)

Cortés landed on Mexican territory in March 1519 and by November of the same year he had seized the Aztec Emperor and held him hostage. After the conquest of Mexico the Spanish conquistadores, maintaining their traditional European eating habits, took across to the New World pigs, chickens, cattle, cereals, vegetables, olive oil, sugar-cane, citrus fruits and wine. After a time

the Mexican Indians started using these ingredients in their native dishes and a new and exciting cuisine was born.

Trade with China and the Philippines was responsible for other additions like rice and spices. Indeed it is said that the 'X' in Mexico appears to embrace food from the four cardinal points. Over the years these influences have culminated in an extraordinary blend of textures, a kaleidoscope of flavours and an extremely nutritious and colourful cuisine.

Independence from Spain

Mexican heroes like Miguel Hidalgo y Costilla (called 'Father of Mexico'), a Creole, the son of Spaniards born in Mexico, and a priest with education, encouraged the natives to plant olives and vines and taught them to read and write and to attain a high standard in music, the arts, metallurgy and other handicrafts. This contradicted the instructions of the Spanish authorities. In 1810, Miguel Hidalgo and a handful of native Indians declared the Mexican War of Independence which brought to an end 300 years of Spanish rule.

The whole country erupted in violence – peaceful, complaisant Indians took whatever weapons they could find and criss-crossed the land, fighting, hiding and camping in unexplored peaceful valleys. The women who followed their men into battle were forced to share culinary secrets and to experiment with new ingredients. They learned of the wide range of chillies and beans and their varied flavours and different uses. In this way the many regional varieties of cooking travelled through Mexico, enriching and enhancing other methods.

When Independence was finally achieved eleven years later, in a country still licking its wounds, a new cuisine had been born which combined the culinary expertise of a millennium of indigenous dishes with centuries-old Spanish traditions, and included dishes and customs from the 800 years of Moorish domination of the Spanish Peninsula.

War with the United States

Mexico's perpetual dictator, Antonio Lopez the Santa Ana, a shifty character, was then in power for thirty years. He won the battle of the Alamo in Texas but lost badly to Sam Houston at San Jacinto in 1836. Ten years later he led the Mexican army into a disastrous war with the United States and lost half his country's territory in the process. Texans hated him and wanted their own independence. This was not achieved because they then became members of the Union. However, Texan–Mexican food established itself firmly in the territory. The other border states of California, Arizona, Utah and New Mexico developed their own styles of Mexican food, which have maintained lasting popularity in that region.

French Invasion

By 1861 Mexico was in deep economic trouble, having to suspend payments to Spain, Britain and France. The French saw this as an opportunity to invade and add Mexico to their overseas empire. Napoleon III named the Archduke of Austria, Ferdinand Maximilian Joseph of Hapsburg, Emperor of Mexico under French protection. In 1863 Maximilian and his wife Carlotta arrived in a hostile and unfriendly kingdom where only a minority were eager to welcome them.

The French occupation came to a sad and

tragic end, but the French influence is noticeable to this day. Dishes like pâté, fricassee, croquettes, crêpes and crème caramel, not to mention an array of delicious breads and sweet cakes, baguettes, brioche, croissants, millefeuilles and many others, are still enjoyed in Mexico. Bread was made with and without eggs and salt, and the art and imagination of the natives was soon manifested in complicated and colourful breads like *pan de muerto* and *rosca de reyes*. Mexican bakery shops are a feast to the eye and it is very difficult to choose from the mouthwatering breads on offer.

The French intervention, brief as it was, had a tremendous influence on the development of Mexican cuisine. In only four years, the French style of cooking invaded Mexico City and was served in all its glory in top society homes, greatly enjoyed by all who had the opportunity to eat it, accompanied, of course, by champagne and French wines. The menus of Mexico were again transformed as the new French style was absorbed into an already rich and exquisite repertoire.

The Mexican Revolution of 1910

Mexico continued to have good and bad times in the second half of the nineteenth century. Porfirio Diaz became President and for the thirty years that he was in power the country settled down to peaceful work. Industry grew rapidly, communications improved, railways connected the remote areas and oil was exploited by powerful British and American companies.

Unfortunately, the position of the Mexican Indians did not improve much. They had more work than before but the gap between the very wealthy and the poor was extremely wide with no middle class to breach it. To end Diaz's thirty-year dictatorship, the guerrilla leader Madero started a revolt in the north soon to be followed by other self-made generals in another cruel civil war out of which Pancho Villa and Emiliano Zapata became legendary revolutionary figures.

Like all revolutions, this war achieved only some of its aims, but again one of the by-products was that regional cooking methods became more and more widely known, as the women continued to support their men by following them into battle, cooking their meals with ingredients they could find at hand, adapting once again to new ideas.

DRINKING HABITS

Largely due to the hot, dry climate, Mexicans have gained quite a reputation for their home-made beverages, alcoholic and otherwise.

Pulque, a drink made from the fermented sap, *agua miel*, extracted from the heart of the agave plant which grows wild, was the only alcoholic drink of the Indian civilisations and it was considered sacred. It is a foamy milky drink with an acrid odour which cannot be disguised even today, despite the efforts of the locals who 'cure' it with fresh fruits like strawberries or pineapple. It has a similar potency to beer and is in fact losing ground to the latter. In modern times it has been found to be slightly hallucinatory.

Tequila, the universally famous Mexican drink, was the product of the imaginative Spaniards who distilled the juice of another type of agave plant, similar to a cactus with which it is often confused. The plant, called *tequilana* or blue mescal, is a member of the amaryllis family with spiky leaves growing straight up from a core close to the ground. It takes 8–14 years to reach maturity and is grown in the land surrounding the township of Tequila in Guadalajara, to the west of Mexico City, from where it takes its name.

When the agave reaches maturity, the plant is cut at the base and all the leaves cut off, leaving the large core which looks like a gigantic pineapple and weighs 25–100 kg

(50–250 lb). The *piñas*, as the cores are called, are steamed until they become soft and stringy, and are then pressed between rollers to extract the juice which is fermented in vats. Distillation begins when fermentation is complete. The tequila is then stored for about three years in wax-lined casks for the transparent colourless drink, and in wooden casks for the *Añejo* (aged) version, which has a golden hue and a mellow flavour. Paper, bricks and fertiliser are produced from the *baggasse* (fibres left after pressing) so little goes to waste.

Mezcal, a fiery alcoholic drink, is produced from the same plant as *tequila* but using different distilling methods. Very few high-quality *mezcals* can be called *tequila,* whilst all *tequilas* are a type of *mezcal*. It has a high alcoholic proof and, to prove it, a small slug is introduced into each bottle and is preserved intact. The faint-hearted, are not advised to try *Mezcal con Gusano,* popularly known as 'tequila with the worm', which is all to be swallowed in one big gulp! It is a talking point at parties and the one brave enough to swallow it is bound to gain applause and admiration. In fact the slug lives on the *tequilana* plant and is considered a gourmet delicacy when deep-fried and served as a filling for warm corn *tortillas* with *gaucamole.*

With the introduction of sugar-cane, rum has become one of Mexico's most popular drinks; both white and dark rums are produced. Mexican wines are excellent and have gained popularity in Europe alongside Californian and Chilean wines. The vine grows well in the northern borderlands.

Beer was introduced to Mexico by the Germans who came to work in the silver and gold mines. It is now the most popular drink in Mexico and Mexican beers have grown in popularity in the rest of the world. They are always offered well chilled, straight from the bottle. It has become fashionable to insert a wedge of lime in the neck of the bottle. This gives the drink a touch of freshness which is welcome on hot summer days. Mexican beer can now be bought in almost all supermarkets and wine shops in the UK.

Fruit drinks are popular with young and old alike. On hot sunny days, as people stroll through the parks, drinks of all colours and fruity flavours can be bought. They are also often served with midday meals. The most popular are freshly squeezed *limonada* (lime-ade) and *agua de Jamaica* (red sorrel flower tea).

'Chocolate' is a word now universally recognised as having its origins in the language of the Aztecs *xoco* meaning 'bitter' and *atl* 'water'. Drinking chocolate is present at many breakfast tables and is enjoyed by most Mexicans – not only by the Emperor and his upper-class nobility as in the old days. It is no longer mixed with water as was the royal custom in pre-Columbian Mexico; it is now dissolved in milk and is usually sweetened with sugar instead of honey. There are several styles of drinking chocolate. The Mexican style – coarsely ground cocoa pods with sugar, cinnamon, cloves and sometimes ground almonds – is an example of the Spanish influence. Vanilla is also often used to flavour chocolate as was the custom before the Conquest. This does not mean Mexicans do not enjoy a bar of chocolate in the same way as it is enjoyed elsewhere in the world.

In addition, chocolate is often used to flavour the pre-Columbian popular drink, *atole*, still enjoyed by the people of today. This consists of *masa* (ground maize) diluted in hot water and sweetened with muscovado sugar. *Atole* is also popular as a savoury drink flavoured with chillies and stock. It is very versatile as it absorbs different flavours to suit all ages. Unfortunately, because it tends to be rich in calories, it has lost favour with the upper classes and it is only prepared for special occasions. This does not apply to the poorer classes, of course.

Café de olla (coffee from the pot), is also well known to most lovers of Mexican food. It is coffee sweetened with muscovado sugar and served with cinnamon syrup (see page 196) instead of cream.

THE FOOD OF MEXICO TODAY

Thanks to the flair and ingenuity of Mexico's cooks, the country's cuisine has become varied and tasty, featuring exciting, colourful dishes with texture and interest. It uses many well-known ingredients and does not require any specific equipment in its preparation.

Communications being what they are, it was no surprise to me to find my friends in Mexico using yoghurt and cottage cheese in their kitchens as well as trying to avoid frying whenever possible. The ideology of 'thin is beautiful' prevails everywhere, with expert cooks creating a 'nouvelle cuisine Mexicaine' in many restaurants and homes. In this book I have introduced these ideas, but my basic objective has been to stay as close as possible to traditional Mexican recipes.

The modern Mexican housewife actually spends little time preparing her own food. This is partly because of the availability of freshly made food and partly because she can employ staff to help her with kitchen duties. There is a multitude of *tortillerías* (tortilla bakeries) and *panaderías* (bakeries) in every neighbourhood and although in the bigger cities the supermarkets have largely replaced the more traditional market-place, a *tortillería* can always be found within walking distance in any suburb in Mexico City. Butchers and milkmen are still willing to deliver to the door for little or no extra cost.

The Markets

In the villages, the markets act as focal points and main meeting places. I spend my time talking to the vendors, observing their customs and their customers. It is here that the art and talent of the land can be appreciated.

In markets throughout Mexico, you can satisfy your appetite at any time of day. For breakfast, after you consume the biggest glass of fresh orange juice you have ever seen, squeezed while you watch, you move on to the lady with a basket filled with freshly made corn *tortillas* and *barbacoa* (steamed lamb) and hot sauce. She prepares soft *tacos* for you, carefully wrapped in a piece of brown paper. If you prefer you can have a *quesadilla* (corn tortilla filled with cheese and potato) or any other filling you fancy, or indeed *enfrijoladas* (corn *tortillas* fried on the underside and topped with refried beans, spicy sausage and sauce). The choice is endless.

Café de olla (coffee), hot chocolate or a mug of *atole*, made with maize and flavoured with fruits or chocolate, are alternative hot drinks which you may enjoy. If you still feel hungry, then a sweet *biscocho* or bun will be ideal to finish this mouthwatering brunch.

If your appetite is small, all you have to do is go shopping. You will find the market vendors are eager to offer portions of their produce for you to taste! If you are lucky you might even get a whole mango as proof that the fruit is sweet and juicy. After this display of generosity, I feel compelled to buy and I always end up with baskets full of fruits I am never able to eat during my short visits.

Entertaining

Entertaining in Mexico is casual and takes place very often. Whole families get together, enabling all ages to mingle. You can do no worse than to arrive at a friend's home whilst they are still eating because you will be sat at the table and offered a full meal even if you've just had one. *Vale mas llegar a tiempo que ser convidado* (it is better to arrive on time than to be invited) is a popular saying and everyone is welcome at a friend's table. The truth is that because Mexicans always have fresh *tortillas* with their meals, it is easy to make the food go further by making the filling for the *tacos* a little smaller.

The setting of the table is formal but simple, the style of eating more in the relaxed French manner. The main Mexican meal takes place at around two o'clock in the afternoon and may last as long as time permits. The meals often take hours with the focus on the savoury dishes rather than on the desserts. Warm *tortillas* are always eaten by hand, even on the most formal of occasions (except when they are covered in a sauce as is the case with *enchiladas*). Raw chopped onions are often used to garnish cooked dishes, and cheese is usually crumbled and in its natural state, rather than melted in the oven.

Freshly made lemonade and beer are always available and black coffee or *café negro* is offered at the end of the meal. Milky coffee and hot chocolate are popular as morning and evening drinks.

Mexican dishes are designed to make meat go a long way and are therefore an economical and healthy way of eating. They can easily be adapted to become interesting vegetarian meals, due to the different flavours and textures and to the large choice of ingredients available. The carbohydrate from the maize, the vitamins from the vegetables, and the protein and fibre from the beans offer a well-balanced daily diet. Mexican food excels in striking the right balance in colour, texture, flavour and nutrition.

I recommend that you make your food slightly hot as people are often disappointed when they are offered Mexican food that isn't. If, however, someone has the misfortune of biting into a hot chilli, offer him or her a piece of Cheddar cheese. This will not only soothe the mouth but will keep the sufferer quiet until the burning subsides!

In the home, the main meal of the day starts with *sopa aguada* (literally translated, this means watery soup), a stock-based dish introduced during colonial days. It is offered hot throughout the year, and despite the heat in the middle of the day, no Mexican menu is complete without it. A good *caldo* or stock can be served as consommé or flavoured with beans, avocados, pumpkin blossoms, dried *tortillas*, rice, pasta or chillies. Warm, freshly made *tortillas* make their appearance at the table at this stage and are eaten throughout the meal.

More unusual is the *sopa seca* or dry soup. This is a pasta or rice dish which is served as a separate course after the *sopa aguada*. The rice is often garnished with sliced avocado, *guacamole* or *salsa ranchera* to give it more flavour. Then, a change of plates and you are offered the main course, for example, a casserole with *tortillas* and meat or a vegetarian *chile relleno* (stuffed pepper) with refried beans. This is followed by a salad and finally a dessert in the shape of fresh fruit, ice cream or crème caramel.

Antojitos, literally 'what you fancy', are hot or cold snacks consumed in Mexico at all times of the day or night. We go so far as to boast that he who doesn't eat *antojitos* between meals is not Mexican. Some *antojitos*, such as *tostadas*, can also be used as a starter to a meal, or they can be served as a main course, like *tamales* or *enchiladas*.

La Copa y la Botana (a drink and a nibble) is offered by Mexican cooks before the meal to stimulate the appetite. At Mexican restaurants you always find *tortilla* chips and *guacamole* or *salsa* to nibble whilst your order is being prepared. It is the equivalent of the Spanish *tapas*.

Mexican hospitality is well known and its secret is the spontaneous offering of food and drink, however humble it might be. This, combined with friendly surroundings and cheerful background music contributes to create the well-known *ambiente Mexicano*.

Entertaining the Mexican way is easy, because the food becomes a good topic of conversation and the tequila will relax the atmosphere even at the most formal of occasions.

INGREDIENTS

The following is a list of ingredients most commonly found in Mexican cooking to help you identify them more easily.

Aniseed
This spice is available from health food shops. It adds flavour to sweet and savoury dishes.

Annatto
This is a small, dark red seed used by the Mayas to colour and flavour their foods. *Achiote* is the name given to the paste consisting of the ground seeds mixed with herbs and oil. It can be purchased as a small block. Its mildly spiced flavour is used for seasoning fish, fowl and meat. Most popular in the Yucatán Peninsula, where the Maya people live, *achiote* paste must be dissolved in Seville orange or grapefruit juice before using. When *achiote* is not available it can be replaced by tandoori mixture from Indian shops, following the instructions on the recipe for *Pollo al Pibil* (see page 128).

Avocado
Aguacates (avocados) are rarely sold ripe, so remember to buy them well in advance. To assist the ripening process, wrap them in newspaper and keep them in a warm place away from direct light and heat. Turn them daily and check them for ripeness by gently pressing them. When they start to soften, put them in the refrigerator to delay further ripening. For *guacamole*, they taste nicer if used when ripe.

Avocados start turning black soon after they are cut, so prepare them at the very last minute. It helps to cover them in lime or lemon juice, with a sprinkling of salt, immediately after cutting them. I prefer the small knobbly-skinned black variety called Hass. I do not recommend the larger round, green, hard-skinned avocados because they have a watery flavour despite their appealing appearance. These should not be confused, however, with the lovely large green avocados that we now find in supermarkets, which are excellent.

In Mexico there is an even smaller variety of *aguacate*, the size of a large plum with a soft, speckly, thin, edible skin which adds to the flavour.

Banana Leaves
Hojas de plátano are not readily available in England, but greaseproof paper and kitchen foil squares are good substitutes. However, should you manage to get some in Soho, from the Asian shops, immerse them in boiling water for 10 minutes to soften them before use, then wrap the food in the leaves to make little parcels and steam them. These leaves are used for the famous *tamales de oaxaca*.

Beans
Frijoles, the staple food of Mexico. There are very many varieties of beans and they are all very good. The most commonly used are the rose-coco (borlotti), turtle beans known as black beans, red kidney and pinto beans. Beans are rich in fibre and protein and well liked for their taste. Black beans are the most difficult to obtain and they must not be

confused with black kidney beans which are larger and less tasty. If canned beans are used, refer to page 30 for their preparation.

Cecina

This dried meat is very similar to the American beef jerky. Other dried meats are suitable substitutes if you cannot obtain it.

Cheese

Queso fresco, queso de Chihuahua, queso de Oaxaca, queso añejo. Queso fresco is used crumbled over raw or cooked hot or cold food. It would be unthinkable to serve *enchiladas* without their crumbled white cheese as garnish. Good substitutes are any of the crumbly white cheeses like Wensleydale, Cheshire or Lancashire. Leave them at room temperature for about an hour and crush them with a fork to a fine crumble.

The arrival of the Menonites in the northern Mexican state of Chihuahua has given birth to the well-known *queso de Chihuahua*, now eaten all over Mexico. It is similar to a mild Cheddar cheese, which can be substituted for it. If using Cheddar I like to mix it with mozzarella to provide the stringy consistency which is a must in Mexican cooked cheese dishes.

I have found that some Italian shops sell what they call *queso pera*, a pear-shaped cheese covered in a layer of transparent wax. This cheese is a good substitute for *queso de Oaxaca* or *queso asadero* used in *quesadillas*.

Queso añejo is an aged cheese which is often called for in *antojitos* and cooked dishes. It is not one of my favourite cheeses; Italian Parmesan can be used instead.

The Mexican cheese industry has grown extensively in the last twenty years and they now produce very acceptable French cheese imitations such as Camembert – delicious with *quesadillas* or *rajas poblanas* instead of Cheddar cheese. There are Mexican varieties of Port Salut, Gruyère, cream cheeses and others.

Chillies

Chiles are the pride and joy of Mexican cuisine as they add colour and flavour to our dishes. They grow abundantly in Mexico and are always available in a variety of sizes, shapes and colours, fresh or dried, pickled or smoked.

Fresh Chillies

Chile de arbol are very thin, long, tight-looking chillies, extremely hot, which come from China. Others, imported from Kenya, are similar to *chile de agua*, more fleshy and less hot. The good news is that I have come across fresh *jalapeños* in the supermarkets, imported from Gambia. They were unusually mild but it all adds to the variety.

Chile Habanero (meaning 'from Habana') is the Caribbean chilli known in England as Scotch bonnet. It has a roundish shape and is sold green, yellow or red. It is considered the hottest chilli of all. Not used in Mexico as much as it is used in the Caribbean Islands, it has a very distinct flavour.

Chile jalapeño is the most popular chilli in the United States, where they use it out of cans. This is because it is very fleshy, about 5 cm (2 inches) long and preserves very well. In Mexico it is also used for pickling. It is available canned or bottled in the United Kingdom.

Chile poblano is a 15–20 cm (6–8 inches) long pointed, hot, dark-green chilli that has yet to

OPPOSITE *Taco* shells (page 74), served with shredded chicken, shredded lettuce, *Guacamole* (avocado dip, page 48) and *Jalapeños en Vinagre* (pickled jalapeño chillies, page 176)

have its debut in European markets. I have to substitute with green peppers for *chiles rellenos* and I confess I put a sliver of *chile de árbol* inside them to achieve a little hotness. If you follow the cooking instructions for this dish you will manage to deceive even trained palates.

Chile serrano is mostly used in cooking. It is about 4 cm (1¹/₂ inches) long and rounded. It is quite hot and can be replaced by the Chinese chillies found in Indian shops.

Dealing with chillies

It is important to remember that chillies are hot, and that the hottest parts are the seeds and veins. Often after just touching a cut chilli your fingers will sting and so will your eyes, nose or any part of you that you happen to touch. Therefore, I strongly recommend using rubber gloves when handling chillies. Cut them on absorbent kitchen paper and wash your knives carefully after use.

Controlling the heat

To guide you in controlling the amount of 'heat' you give a dish, I emphasise that tasting as you cook is most important. Remember that people may insist that they love hot food but scarcely know what they are letting themselves in for. As a general guide, I suggest:

1. To flavour without hotness, add whole chillies during cooking and remove and discard them immediately after.

2. To give more 'heat', cut chillies in half and remove and discard the seeds.

3. For full 'heat', chop the chillies, seeds and all, and add them to the dish. If you taste and the food is not hot enough, just add more chillies until it tastes how you like it. Add small amounts of chillies at a time and taste. If you are not sure how hot your guests will be able to take it, serve some *jalapeños en vinagre* in a small bowl and leave them on the table for people to help themselves once you have explained to them how hot they are.

Suppressing the 'burn'

Notice I call it 'burn' because that is just how it feels when you bite into a hot chilli! It is awful to bite into a chilli by mistake as it can give you a nasty shock. Nothing will really take the burn away immediately, your eyes will fill with tears, your nose will run, you will feel like screaming and might even develop hiccups. I find that chewing a piece of cheese is more effective than drinking gallons of water! But . . . the burn certainly lasts for a long time. The good news is that instead of putting you off chillies entirely, strangely enough it makes you want to try them again. The next time your tolerance will be that much greater and you will be able to appreciate what chillies do for your food.

To keep chillies fresh

Remove the stems carefully and wrap the chillies in a paper bag inside a polythene bag, then seal and refrigerate. They will keep for about two weeks.

I have not been successful in freezing chillies whole, although dishes cooked with chillies in them do not lose their sting. In fact, in some cases, freezing enhances the flavour.

Dried Chillies

Dried chillies are found in the Mexican markets at all times of the year, although traditionally they were dried to provide sustenance for the winter months when the earth was dry. *Chile ancho* is particularly rich in vitamin A; it

OPPOSITE Left to right: *Faisán al Achiote* (pheasant in anatto sauce, page 126) and *Budín de Camote* (sweet potato purée, page 154)

is occasionally possible to find it in Europe in specialist shops.

Chiles secos is the general term for the wide variety of dried chillies, each with a distinctive flavour and colour to enhance the simplest of sauces. They are all compatible with one another, thus giving the aficionado the opportunity of preparing umpteen sauce combinations. The most commonly used are *chile ancho, chile mulato, chile pasilla, chile chilpotle, chile guajillo* and *chile cascabel.* It needs an expert eye to distinguish the *ancho* from the *mulato* but if you hold them to the light you can see a reddish hue in the *chile ancho* and a definite blackness in the *mulato. Pasilla* is less hot, sweeter, long and black, often cut into fine slices, fried, and used as a garnish for soups.

Chile chilpotle is the dried version of the fresh *jalapeño.* It is smoked and gives food a distinct barbecued taste.

Guajillo is orange-red, smooth-skinned and pointed, similar to the Californian Anaheim but hotter.

Cascabel takes its name from the rattle the seeds make when the chilli is shaken. It often accompanies *barbacoa.*

Chocolate

Chocolate was considered the drink of the gods. To this day it is more popular in Mexico as a drink than as a confection. Unsweetened cooking chocolate, made the Mexican way, is an acceptable substitute.

Chorizo

Chorizo is a Spanish spicy pork sausage. It is very popular in Mexico with eggs or as a garnish for *Antojitos.* It can be bought in delicatessens and supermarkets, and a recipe appears on page 142.

Christophine or Cho-Cho

Chayote is a heart-shaped vegetable, light green in colour, about 13 cm (5 inches) long. Its flavour is watery and earthy and it can be obtained from Indian or West Indian shops. The best quality is the Mexican dark green extremely prickly *chayote*, which is boiled in the skin and peeled before serving.

Cinnamon

Canela is used in sticks, although ground cinnamon is an excellent substitute. Use 1 teaspoon ground cinnamon for each 5 cm (2 inches) cinnamon stick.

Coffee

Café is drunk in Mexico most of the time, although herbal teas are becoming increasingly popular. Mexicans enjoy coffee black, with milk or with cinnamon syrup as *café de olla* (see page 196).

Cooking Fats

Manteca (pork fat) is widely used in Mexico for frying. *Antojitos* cooked in pork fat taste better too, but with health in mind I have substituted unsaturated oil for animal fat in the recipes in this book. I particularly like corn oil. Remember never to start frying in cold or lukewarm oil; always heat it up first. Drain excess fat from foods on kitchen paper towels.

Coriander (fresh)

Cilantro or *culantro* is used raw in vast amounts. This herb indisputably adds the magic to some Mexican dishes. It has no substitute when called for in raw sauces or *guacamole* – it is better to do without than to substitute. Occasionally, when a substitute is acceptable, I have mentioned it. Fresh coriander is sold in most supermarkets as well as in Indian, West Indian and Greek shops. It keeps well for about ten days in the refrigerator if you cut off the roots, wrap it lightly in absorbent kitchen paper and keep it in a sealed plastic container. It loses its flavour when frozen. It can be grown from seed in a semi-sunny position.

Corn (sweetcorn)

Elote is used as a vegetable and is found fresh in Mexican markets the whole year round. However, frozen corn kernels are a good substitute when fresh corn is not available. There are white, yellow, blue and red corn varieties.

Corn Husks

Hojas para tamal, like *hojas de plátano*, are used as wrappers when steaming food. These are the outer leaves of corn on the cob. They are used to make *tamales* and can usually be bought ready dried. They are not edible. You can substitute squares of waxed (not grease-proof) paper inside squares of kitchen foil for the husks, but you will lose a little flavour.

Courgettes

Calabacitas are of two basic shapes in Mexico: the rounded ones are young spaghetti squash or pumpkin, and the longer ones are the young marrows available in this country.

Courgette Blossoms

Flores de calabaza are the blossoms from courgette, pumpkin or marrow plants, and are seldom found in the shops. I wait until my plants have pollinated and then carefully remove and freeze the blossoms until I have enough to cook as filling for *tacos* or *quesadillas*.

Cream (soured)

Crema agria is called for in some of the recipes. If you wish to make your own, add 1 teaspoon lime or lemon juice to 150 ml ($^1/_4$ pint) single cream and allow it to stand for 20 minutes. Otherwise, the commercial varieties of soured cream are very good.

Cuitlacoche (huitlacoche)

This Mexican delicacy can be bought fresh or canned in Mexico. It is a fungus that grows on corn on the cob and deforms the kernel. It has a mushroomy flavour and is almost black when cooked.

Epazote

This herb is used in Mexico as much as the Italians use oregano. An aromatic herb, it is used to flavour soups, stews and beans. It is always used fresh but I have found dried *epazote* quite successful. I have grown it in my garden in a shady, humid position. It is a perennial so it comes back every year. It can also be found in Spain and Portugal.

Green Tomatillos

Tomates verdes are not to be confused with ordinary green tomatoes. These are a relation of the cape gooseberry (physallis) and turn yellow when ripe. They have a transparent, loose husk which must be removed before cooking. Tomatillos have no adequate substitute, but can occasionally be found in supermarkets and are available canned. You can grow your own from seeds purchased from seed merchants under the name of 'sugar giant'.

Hominy

Maiz cacahuazintle are very large, dried corn kernels which are used for *pozole* and other dishes. They require soaking before use. Hominy is available from health food shops.

Jícama

A large brown-skinned tuber shaped like a flat turnip, *jícama* is eaten raw, with its thin brown skin peeled off. It is used as a *botana* with drinks, thinly sliced and sprinkled with lime, salt and cayenne pepper.

Masa Harina (maize meal)

Masa harina is a specially treated flour used to make corn *tortillas* and *tamales*. It may also be used to thicken sauces. It is made from yellow, white or blue corn. It has no substitute and is very fine and powdery. Ordinary yellow cornmeal will not make *tortillas*. To make your own, see page 23, but I advise buying it.

Mole or Molli

This is the name given to the most traditional Mexican sauce which is usually served with turkey, pork or chicken. It is a combination of different chillies, spices, nuts and bitter chocolate simmered together with the cooked meat and its stock. Its flavour is unique. *Mole* powder is a practical way of buying the ingredients already blended. *Mole* paste is *mole* powder in an oily base.

A poor substitute for *mole* powder is 1 tablespoon of ground chilli powder mixed with 1 teaspoon cornflour for every 50 g (2 oz) chillies, or for every two dried chillies called for in your recipe.

Nopales

This is the Spanish name for paddle cactus, the fleshy leaves of the prickly pear plant (paddle cactus). They can be bought cleaned with all the sharp thorns cut off. The younger the paddles the better. They are more popular than ever now because they add variety to salads and cooked dishes and are excellent in calorie-controlled diets.

Paw-Paw

Papaya is a large elongated melon-shaped fruit, green and yellow skinned, with an orange fleshy inside. It is often served as a

starter or for breakfast. In England, tiny paw-paw can be found in supermarkets, often with a good flavour, especially when served with a squeeze of lime juice.

Pecan Nuts

Nueces encarceladas have become well known in England. They are like elongated walnuts and are very popular in American cookery. They grow abundantly in Mexico and, like walnuts, are used for cooking.

Plantain

Plátano macho are large bananas which cannot be eaten raw. They must be very ripe to use in Mexican cooking. They are sold in West Indian shops and markets, and can be boiled, roasted or fried.

Pulses

Lentejas y garbanzos are the other pulses used in Mexico alongside beans. They are cooked in exactly the same manner as beans and then seasoned according to the recipe.

Pumpkin

Calabaza grows in the British Isles very successfully. It is large, round and deep yellow. In Mexico it is not used as a vegetable but is very popular as a dessert stewed with raw sugar, cinnamon and orange rind.

Pumpkin Seeds

Pepitas can be found in most food shops. In Mexico they are roasted and salted before being sold. You peel each *pepita* as you go along. They are also peeled, dry-fried and salted and offered as an appetiser instead of peanuts. Lastly, they are used in savoury dishes or as a thickening agent.

Rice

Arroz was introduced into Mexico by Spain. The type used is normally the long-grain white rice found in most supermarkets. I prefer the

shop's own brand to the boxed type which I find is very starchy. Should you prefer to use the boxed variety, I recommend that, before cooking, you rinse it under hot running water for a minute to remove some of the extra starch that can make the rice sticky.

Sesame Seeds

Ajonjolí is a fine seed, used as garnish and in small amounts in sauces. They can be obtained from health food shops and supermarkets.

Shrimps (dried)

Camarón seco can be bought peeled and cleaned from Chinese shops. They have a strong flavour and go well with rice.

Sweet Buns

Biscochos are similar to Bath buns, Swiss rolls, etc. *Pan de muerto, campechanas* or *rosca de reyes* are usually offered with hot chocolate.

Sweet Potatoes

Camotes are large tubers similar to large redskinned potatoes but not of the same family. They can be boiled or baked in their skins and their sweet flesh used as a vegetable or dessert.

Tomatoes

Jitomates are large and irregularly shaped in Mexico. They have a stronger flavour and are sold ripe but firm. I like to buy beef tomatoes for salads when available, but in England I do not buy fresh tomatoes for cooking because they are very expensive. I prefer canned peeled tomatoes which are inexpensive and convenient.

Tortillas (corn)

These are now available fresh in supermarket bakery departments, and can also be bought frozen. I would rather do without than use the canned variety.

Tortillas (wheat)

Now widely available in large supermarkets. However, they are not difficult to make and I strongly recommend you make your own (see page 26) as the ingredients are available and a little determination will produce good results.

Vinegar (malt)

Vinagre is widely used in Mexico for seasoning meats and for adding a little sharpness to sauces and soups. English vinegar is stronger than that used in Mexico. I do not mind the difference but if you find it too strong, dilute it half-and-half with water. Distilled vinegar is better for pickles because it does not discolour the vegetables.

BASIC RECIPES

IN MEXICO, it is not essential to anticipate your cooking requirements; most ingredients can be found at any time of the year, whether they are strictly in season or not. *Tortillas* are available freshly made every day from the *tortillerías*, small bakeries found on every street corner which are open seven days a week. Sunday markets also provide a wonderful variety of delicacies, which often differ from those found during the week. Moreover, many Mexican homes have a maid who buys, prepares and serves every meal, and then clears up afterwards.

Outside Mexico, especially in Europe, the picture is very different. For this reason I supply in this chapter basic recipes which can be cooked in volume and then frozen or refrigerated. Frozen *tortillas* and ready-to-use *salsas* turn a simple meal into a Mexican gourmet's delight with ease.

The food often improves with keeping. This is especially true in the case of *molli* sauce and beans, both of which freeze very well. The cooked tomato sauce is good not only for *huevos rancheros, pescado a la Veracruzana, chiles rellenos* and *enchiladas,* but I also use it to make Mexican pizzas, spaghetti bolognese, soups and stews.

The mainstay of the Mexican meal are corn *tortillas,* beans and chillies. Clear stocks are very much a part of Mexican food prepa-

ration; soups are a must at the beginning of a meal and they are usually meat-stock based. Adding chillies to food can cause problems because some people can tolerate higher levels of 'hotness' than others. To avoid serving food that is too hot for some people, Mexican homes serve very hot sauces and pickled chillies separately, so that extra 'heat' can be added by those who enjoy it.

The native peoples of each country have passed down valuable secrets from generation to generation which unfortunately, in our modern times, are being lost despite their efficacy. How did the Mexican natives find out that they needed to add limestone to the corn before preparing it for their *tortillas?* Was it just coincidence or did they actually know that if they didn't, they would suffer a calcium deficiency, their teeth and bones would weaken, and their minds would get confused? How long did this method of making *tortillas* take to develop? These questions must now go unanswered, but the Mexican Indian has avoided suffering from any calcium deficiency or malnutrition as a result.

Fresh corn *tortillas* are made from fresh *masa* which can be made at home. However, I do not recommend that you start doing this if you have never before made your own. Buying commercially produced *masa harina* is a much better alternative. If this is not possible, however, you might feel tempted to start from scratch. You can obtain garden lime from any garden centre or gardening shop but try to obtain food-grade lime to ensure it does not contain any other additives.

Masa Harina

MAIZE MEAL

MAKES 1 kg (2 lb) *Masa*

INGREDIENTS

1 kg (2 lb) dried corn kernels	50 g (2 oz) garden lime
3 litres (6 pints) water	

METHOD

■ Wash the maize kernels and place them in a large saucepan with the water. Dissolve the lime in a little cold water and strain the liquid into the pan. Bring the contents to the boil, cover and simmer for 30 minutes. Remove from the heat, drain and allow to cool.

■ When cool enough to handle comfortably, rub the kernels between your hands and remove the outer skin and any 'eyes' (the 'pin-pricks' at the end of each kernel). Rinse the meal in cold water to remove any bits left behind, and to wash off the lime.

■ Place about 5 tablespoons of meal at a time in a blender and blend to a smooth paste. (The electric blender avoids the arduous task of kneeling down with a *metate* and grinding by hand!) Continue blending in small amounts until all the meal is done. You now have ready-mixed *masa* which can be used for *tortillas de maiz* or *antojitos.*

Tortillas de Maiz

CORN *TORTILLAS*

〜〜

*T*ortillas are the most typical of all Mexican foods, and the most versatile. They can be used in starters, soups, main courses and even desserts. We eat them in between meals, by themselves if freshly made, with dips, sauces, meats, salads, cheese and even ham, but we never eat them cold (unless, of course, they are golden-fried and crispy)!

Making your own *tortillas* is fun, but not easy. You need a *tortilla* press, a griddle and waxed paper (not greaseproof paper) squares. (Waxed paper can be bought from stationery shops.) However, if you follow this recipe carefully you will reap rewards. *Tortillas* are becoming more and more popular and can now be bought ready-made at some delicatessens and supermarkets. This recipe makes about forty-five *tortillas*, each about 13 cm (5 inches) in diameter. You may make them bigger or smaller, as you wish. This dough is also used for making *atole*, *tamales*, and some *antojitos*. To freeze, just wrap the *tortillas* in a polythene bag and seal. To refrigerate, keep them airtight at about 4°C for up to two weeks. I do not recommend freezing the ready-made dough (*masa*) because it becomes less maleable and impossible to handle.

INGREDIENTS

750 g (1¹/₂ lb) *masa harina* (see page 19)	SPECIAL EQUIPMENT
175 g (6 oz) plain flour	griddle or heavy-based frying pan
750 ml (1¹/₄ pints) warm water	forty-five 15 cm (6 inch) squares of waxed (not greaseproof) paper
	1 **tortilla** press
	2 clean tea-towels

METHOD

■ Mix the flours together in a bowl. Using an electric mixer with a dough hook, continue mixing at low speed while adding the warm water gradually until the mixture sticks together, leaving the sides of the bowl absolutely clean. This takes about 10 minutes. (If this process is done by hand, treat as for bread dough and knead for about 20 minutes.)

■ If the sides of the bowl are sticky, add a little more flour or *masa harina* and carry on mixing. (You cannot overmix *masa*.) Test the dough by squeezing it between two fingers. If cracks appear, the dough is too dry, so add a little more water, mix and test again. As you gain expertise you will learn to make slight adjustments according to the humidity of the room, the age of the flour and the temperature. The dough is ready for use when a small ball immersed in a glass of cold water does not dissolve. Keep the dough covered with a damp tea-towel while you press out all the *tortillas*.

■ Heat a dry griddle or heavy-based frying pan until a few drops of water sizzle on it. Meanwhile, open the *tortilla* press and place a square of waxed paper on its base, shiny side up. Take a small amount of dough, the size of a plum, and roll it in your hands, flattening it to make a thick round about 4 cm ($1^1/_2$ inches) in diameter. Lay this on the waxed paper, about 1 cm ($^1/_2$ inch) closer to the bracket than to the centre of the press. Now place another square of waxed paper on top of the dough, shiny side down. Close the lid of the *tortilla* press and apply gentle pressure to the lever, holding the base of the lever with your left hand. The *tortilla* should flatten easily; if it doesn't the dough is too dry! When flat, it should be about as thin as a penny. It will thicken slightly as it cooks. You will learn how much pressure you need to apply when you have done a few.

■ Reduce the heat slightly. Holding the two squares of paper with the flattened *tortilla* in one hand, carefully peel off the top layer of waxed paper with your other hand, keeping your hand close to the paper and taking care not to tear the dough. You are now holding in your hand a perfectly round, smooth *tortilla* stuck to a square of waxed paper.

■ Gradually lower the *tortilla*, exposed side down, on to the hot griddle, leaving the top waxed paper in place. To avoid trapping air, start by placing the *tortilla* from the side nearest to your little finger and letting go gently. After about 1 minute, the top waxed paper will have loosened and can easily be peeled off. The paper can be re-used successfully several times. Within about 2 minutes, as the *tortilla* cooks, the edges will start to lift away from the griddle. Using a spatula, turn the *tortilla* and cook for 40 seconds. Turn again and cook for a further 30 seconds. If it fluffs up as you touch it with the spatula while it is still cooking after the third turn, you can congratulate yourself – you have produced a perfect *tortilla*. If, on the other hand, it does not puff up, don't be disheartened – practice makes perfect and even I had a hard time learning. Repeat until the dough is finished.

■ As the *tortillas* are cooked, stack them on a wire rack, wrapped in a clean tea-towel. This prevents them from drying. The *tortillas* are now ready to be eaten but they can be stored in a sealed polythene bag in the refrigerator for up to 10 days, or frozen for up to 6 months. *Tortillas* always fry better when they are a day old.

■ In Mexico *tortillas* are reheated in the kitchen whilst you are sitting at the table and brought to the dining-room in small quantities in order to keep them warm at all times. I find this impossible to do in England so you are best advised to reheat as follows.

■ Microwave 12 *tortillas* at a time in a sealed polythene bag for 1 minute only on High (100%). Any longer seems to make them chewy.

■ To reheat them in a conventional oven, wrap 12 *tortillas* carefully in kitchen foil and place in a hot oven (230°C, 450°F, Gas Mark 8) for 10 minutes. As you get one pack out, replace with another so that you can serve hot *tortillas* throughout the meal.

■ To reheat them on a griddle or in a heavy-based frying pan, stack about 8 *tortillas* on top of each other on a very hot griddle. Cover them with a lid for 20 seconds, then uncover and turn them over so that the bottom ones are on the top. Repeat until all the *tortillas* feel hot.

Tortillas de Harina

(WHEAT FLOUR *TORTILLAS*)

MAKES 14
25cm (10 inch)
tortillas

Wheat flour *tortillas* are probably more popular outside Mexico than corn *tortillas* because their flavour is similar to pastry. Wheat flour *tortillas* can be used in exactly the same way as corn *tortillas* but they are more brittle when deep-fried. I have discovered innumerable uses for this type of *tortilla*: it makes *burritos* and *chimichangas*; can be used instead of crêpes, pasta or pie pastry; and makes a pizza base with excellent results. For convenience, I serve them instead of chapatis with curry. I also make Chinese crispy rolls or 'doilies' for Peking duck. They fry into fabulous shapes and can be used for starters, main courses or desserts. To refrigerate, keep them stacked in a sealed polythene bag for up to 2 weeks, but if you wish to freeze them, use waxed paper to separate them because they stick together.

Wholemeal flour can be used for this recipe with identical results and a more nutritious *tortilla*. More filling than corn *tortillas* because of the fat content, they are easier to make in that you do not require special equipment. A good rolling pin and strong determination usually win the round. When freshly cooked, these *tortillas* should be floppy and supple; it is easy to make them brittle by overcooking them.

The size of wheat *tortillas* may vary with the region. In Mexico City we like them 15–18 cm (6–7 inches) in diameter, further north they make them 20–23 cm (8–9 inches) in diameter, while in the United States 25 cm (10 inches) is the most popular *tortilla* size, with some exceptions which are even larger.

INGREDIENTS

500 g (1¼ lb) plain white or wholemeal flour	75 g (3 oz) lard, cubed
1 tablespoon salt	300 ml (½ pint) hot water

METHOD

■ Put the dry ingredients in a mixing bowl, add the fat and rub it in until the mixture resembles breadcrumbs. (An electric mixer or food processor makes this job easier, particularly if you wish to double the recipe.) Mix in the hot water to make a soft, warm pliable dough.

■ Turn the dough on to a floured surface and knead until no longer sticky. Cover with a warm, damp tea-towel.

■ Shape about 50 g (2 oz) dough into a ball the size of a plum, then flatten it. Place on a floured board, and with a floured rolling pin roll it out until it is thin enough to see the board through the pastry. (This requires determination and gets easier with experience.)

■ If your *tortilla* is not perfectly round, don't worry. Cheat, like I do, and trim the *tortilla* to an even shape by cutting round a dinner plate of the desired size. Carry on rolling and cutting the *tortillas*, putting them on a floured tray when rolled, and making sure there is enough flour on them to stop them sticking together. Don't stack more than two high whilst they are raw.

■ Heat a dry griddle or heavy-based frying pan until a few drops of water sizzle on it, then reduce the heat to moderate. Pick up a *tortilla* and place it carefully on the hot griddle. Leave it for about 30 seconds; as it cooks it will thicken a little. When it starts to bubble, turn it over and cook for a further 10 seconds. At this stage the *tortilla* will have lost its transparency, but will still look very pale. This does not matter, as it will cook a little more when you warm it up. If you overcook it, it will become dry and brittle and will not be supple enough to fold. Stack the *tortillas* on a wire rack, wrapped in a clean tea-towel.

■ When all the *tortillas* are cooked and cool, place a square of waxed paper between each one to prevent them from sticking together. Store in a sealed polythene bag. Wheat *tortillas* should be reheated in the same way as corn *tortillas* (see page 26). Never eat them cold, except when they have been deep-fried or baked dry in the oven.

Frijoles

---- BEANS ----

SERVES 8

Beans are delicious and nutritious. They contribute valuable protein, iron and fibre to the diet and a great majority of Mexicans eat them at every meal. They make delicious soups, main courses and side dishes. They are used as a spread instead of butter, and the connoisseur will like them refried.

Beans must be cleaned, washed and soaked, then cooked at a rolling boil for at least 15 minutes in order to neutralise the gasses they contain. A most important rule to remember is *never* to add cold water to them while they are cooking. Always add boiling water.

Beans are at their best eaten one or two days after cooking. They keep well in the refrigerator for up to 8 days and longer if refried often. They heat up easily in the microwave and are an excellent stand-by. Because of the lengthy initial cooking time, it is a good idea to cook more than you need for one meal, say 450 g (1 lb) at a time; this will feed about eight people, or six if the beans are to be refried. They freeze extremely well. Mexicans cook their beans at a rolling boil for the whole of the cooking time. If you are in a hurry, you can cook them in 45 minutes in a pressure cooker. Follow the manufacturer's instructions.

INGREDIENTS

450 g (1 lb) dried black, pinto, red kidney or borlotti beans	2 teaspoons salt
	2 teaspoons sugar
2 cloves garlic, skewered on a cocktail stick for easy removal	2 tablespoons oil
	1 onion, chopped
1 onion, cut in half	
4 green chillies	

METHOD

■ Examine the beans and remove any stones or unwanted bits carefully. Place them in a large sieve and rinse them under cold running water for several minutes, until the water runs clear. Place the clean beans in a saucepan and cover them with enough fresh cold water to come about 15 cm (6 inches) above the top of the beans. Leave them to soak overnight; they will double in size.

■ Next day, top up the pan with more water and add the garlic, halved onion and two whole chillies. Bring to the boil and cook, partly covered, for about 3 hours or until the beans feel very soft between the fingers. Top up with boiling water frequently during cooking (never use cold water). When the beans are soft, discard the garlic, cocktail sticks, onion and chillies, and add the salt and sugar. Simmer gently for 10 minutes.

■ Heat the oil in a frying pan and fry the chopped onion until golden. Add the oil, onion and remaining chillies to the beans, and simmer for 15 minutes or until the bean liquid thickens. To hasten this process, you can mash a few beans against the side of the pan. Cool, cover and refrigerate for 2 weeks or freeze for up to 3 months.

Shortcuts to Cooking Beans

If you haven't got time to soak the beans overnight, then examine, wash, rinse and cover them with cold water as if they are going to be soaked, but put them on to cook. Bring them to the boil quickly and allow them to boil rapidly for 15 minutes. Switch off the heat, cover the beans and leave them to stand for about 2 hours. After this time you can proceed with the normal cooking process as in the recipe above, but the cooking time will be reduced considerably.

Using Canned Beans

SERVES 8

Since I wrote my first book in 1983, a good variety of canned beans has appeared on the supermarket shelves. If time is at a premium, bought canned beans will improve in flavour if treated in the following way.

INGREDIENTS

2 tablespoons oil	2 green chillies, chopped
1 onion, finely chopped	¹/₂ teaspoon sugar
2 cloves garlic, crushed	¹/₂ teaspoon salt
four 400 g (14 oz) cans borlotti or red kidney beans	

METHOD

■ Heat the oil in a frying pan and fry the onion and garlic until golden. Add the beans and their liquid and the remaining ingredients. Simmer over medium heat until the liquid is reduced and the consistency of the beans is that of thick porridge.

Frijoles Refritos

REFRIED BEANS

SERVES 4

Refried beans are an acquired taste. They are beans which have been dehydrated by frying, so the flavour is much more accentuated and unique. The only disadvantage to offering them to untrained palates is their texture – they are similar to mashed potatoes but much dryer. In my experience, the average European prefers beans whole and not quite so dry, so I serve them with another dish with plenty of sauce.

Refried beans must be mashed into a purée. You can either mash them with a potato masher while they are frying, which is the traditional way, or purée them beforehand in a food processor or blender.

INGREDIENTS

2 tablespoons oil	8 *Totopos* (see page 46), optional
¹/₂ onion, quartered	3 tablespoons Wensleydale cheese, finely crumbled
¹/₂ quantity cooked Frijoles (see page 28)	
GARNISH	
¹/₂ onion, finely chopped	

METHOD

■ Heat the oil in a heavy-based frying pan and fry the onion quarters until black. Remove from the pan and discard. Add the beans and fry over medium heat, stirring frequently and mashing as you go along. If the beans stick to the sides of the pan, scrape them off as you stir. If they stick to the bottom, you might need to add a little more oil to the centre of the pan, allowing it to heat up before mixing it into the beans.

■ The consistency of the beans will become thicker as they fry. When they are as thick as porridge, they are ready for spreading on *burritos*, *tostadas* or *tortas*, or for serving as a side dish. If you like them truly refried, then carry on stirring and frying until they stick together like a paste and you can toss them in the air and catch them again in the frying pan, like a pancake. Garnish with any or all of the garnishes and eat hot. Should you wish to refry these beans again, add some water to soften them before proceeding as above. They will freeze and microwave well.

Maiz Cacahuazintle

HOMINY

MAKES about
450 g (1 lb)

This is a special large type of white maize. When cooked, the kernels burst and resemble flowers. In Mexico, this type of maize is used in soups but it is necessary to discard the skins and the heads first.

It is possible to find canned *maiz cacahuazintle* (hominy). Otherwise, you will need to use dried maize kernels and garden lime (see pages 22–3). Preparation starts 2 days in advance.

INGREDIENTS

500 g (1¼ lb) dried corn kernels	1 teaspoon garden lime
1.5 litres (2½ pints) cold water	

METHOD

■ Wash the maize kernels and soak them in cold water overnight. Drain, place in a saucepan with more cold water, and bring to the boil. Reduce the heat and simmer for about 2 hours. Dilute the lime in a little cold water, strain on to the maize, and boil for 10 minutes. Remove from the heat, cover and leave for about 1 hour.

■ Drain and wash the kernels in warm water three or four times. Rub the kernels between your thumbs and forefingers to peel off the transparent skin. If the 'pin-prick' base is still attached, cut that off as well. Rinse again and use or freeze.

Salsa de Tomate Verde

GREEN TOMATILLO SAUCE

MAKES
600 ml (1 pint);
enough for 10
tamales

Despite their similar names, tomatoes and *tomatillos* come from different plant families. The *tomatillo* is related to the cape gooseberry or physallis fruit; its taste is distinctly different from that of a green tomato. It is covered with a thin papery husk and is yellow, not red, when ripe. With the popularity of Mexican food growing around the world, I hope it will soon be easy to find fresh *tomatillos* at most greengrocers. If you miss them, you can grow your own; seeds are available from seed-merchants under the name of 'New Sugar Giant'. *Salsa de Tomate Verde* is used for *tacos, mollis* like *pipian, tamales*, stews and other savoury dishes. This recipe makes enough *salsa* for about ten *tamales*. It freezes and microwaves well.

INGREDIENTS

two 275 g (10 oz) cans green *tomatillos* or 450 g (1 lb) fresh tomatillos, husked

1 tablespoon oil

1/2 onion, charred and chopped (see page 43)

1 clove garlic, charred and crushed (see page 43)

12 sprigs fresh coriander

1/4 teaspoon ground black pepper

pinch of dried oregano

1/4 teaspoon salt

METHOD

■ If using fresh *tomatillos*, put them in a saucepan with a little water, and simmer for 5 minutes. Drain and reserve the water. Meanwhile, heat the oil in a heavy-based frying pan and fry the onion and garlic for 4 minutes. In a blender, purée the cooked fresh or canned tomatillos with their liquid and the remaining ingredients. Add the purée to the frying pan and simmer for about 25 minutes or until it starts to thicken.

Salsa de Jitomate Típica

UNCOOKED TOMATO SALSA

SERVES 4

Salsa is the life of any Mexican dish. It enlivens refried beans; garnishes *tostadas* or taco shells; provides welcome moisture to warm *tortillas*; and is so very easy to make. This sauce is the simplest of them all and forms the basis of more complicated *salsas* involving additional ingredients and different cooking methods.

INGREDIENTS

4 medium-sized ripe but firm tomatoes, chopped	juice of $1/2$ lemon
8 sprigs fresh coriander, finely chopped	$1/2$ teaspoon salt
$1/4$ onion, finely chopped	$1/4$ teaspoon ground black pepper
2 green chillies, finely chopped	

METHOD

■ Mix all the ingredients together and marinate for about 15 minutes before serving.

Salsa de Jitomate Asado

GRILLED TOMATO SAUCE

SERVES 4

This sauce is used in the same way as *Salsa Típica*, but it has a smoother texture. Grilling the tomatoes to char them before peeling adds flavour.

INGREDIENTS

4 medium-sized ripe but firm tomatoes, charred and peeled	$1/4$ onion, charred and quartered
2 green chillies, punctured with a fork, charred and stalks removed	juice of $1/2$ lemon
	$1/2$ teaspoon salt
8 sprigs fresh coriander	$1/4$ teaspoon ground black pepper

METHOD

■ Blend all the ingredients at high speed in a blender or food processor for 30 seconds. Keep refrigerated until required. If you prefer, pound the tomatoes and chillies together with a pestle and mortar, finely chop the coriander and the onion, and add the other ingredients. This sauce must be eaten within 2 hours of preparation.

Salsa de Jitomate

COOKED TOMATO SAUCE

MAKES 1 litre
(1³/₄ pints)

If you have read the two previous recipes for *salsa*, you will have noticed that we are progressing in the method of cooking. From raw to grilled, to boiled. This *salsa* is the base of most Mexican sauces and indeed of many Mexican dishes. It is simple to make, light and tasty. I use it for breakfast, lunch or dinner dishes. It is a good stand-by sauce to keep in the freezer ready to give a boost to *chilaquiles, huevos rancheros, enchiladas*, etc.

In Mexico, tomatoes are very large and dark red as well as very inexpensive. In Europe, canned peeled tomatoes are a good substitute because they have been allowed to ripen on the plant. Bulgarian canned tomatoes have the added benefit of having had their skins removed by charring which makes them more flavourful. This recipe makes enough for twelve *enchiladas*.

INGREDIENTS

2 tablespoons oil	2 green chillies, punctured with a fork
1 onion, charred and finely chopped (see page 43)	two 500 g (1¹/₄ lb) cans peeled tomatoes
	4 sprigs fresh coriander
1 clove garlic, charred and crushed (optional) (see page 43)	¹/₄ teaspoon ground black pepper

METHOD

■ Heat the oil in a heavy-based frying pan and sauté the onion, garlic and chillies for 3 minutes. Mash the tomatoes with their juice and add to the pan with the remaining ingredients. Simmer for about 20 minutes or until the chillies are a dull green colour and soft, and the mixture has thickened. Discard the coriander sprigs and the chillies. Serve hot or cold.

VARIATION

For a hot version of the sauce, chop up the chillies and return them to the sauce.

SALSA PARA ENCHILADAS (Smooth Enchilada Sauce) Unlike the recipe above, in which the sauce is required to have texture, *enchilada* sauce is often preferred very smooth. To achieve this, blend all the ingredients, except the chillies, at high speed for a few seconds, and then fry in the hot oil. Add the chillies and simmer for about 20 minutes. Remove the chillies from the sauce before serving, or chop and return them to the sauce if a hotter flavour is preferred.

Salsa de Jitomate de Bote

—— SMOOTH *ENCHILADA* SAUCE MADE WITH TOMATO PURÊE ——

MAKES 900 ml (1¹/₂ pints); enough for 12 *enchiladas*

INGREDIENTS

1 clove garlic, charred (see page 43)	6 sprigs fresh coriander
1 onion, charred and quartered (see page 43)	1 tablespoon oil
350 g (12 oz) tomato purée	1 litre (1³/₄ pints) water
2 green chillies	¹/₂ teaspoon salt
	¹/₄ teaspoon ground black pepper

METHOD

■ Blend the first five ingredients until smooth. Heat the oil in a deep saucepan, add the mixture and sauté for 3 minutes. Add the water, salt and black pepper. Simmer gently for 20 minutes or until the sauce thickens to the consistency of single cream. Serve hot or cold.

Salsa Adobada

—— DRIED *CHILE ANCHO* SAUCE ——

MAKES 600 ml (1 pint) enough for 10 tamales

This is one of the many versions of *salsa* that can be used with any dish in Mexican cooking. It is relatively quick and very tasty. It makes a good barbecue sauce for spare ribs or a base for *Chilli con Carne*. It is worthwhile remembering that all varieties of dried chillies can be intermingled; they all need treating in a similar manner and the combinations of flavours add interest to the food.

INGREDIENTS

3 cloves garlic, charred (see page 43)	1 tablespoon finely grated cooking chocolate
¹/₂ teaspoon ground cinnamon	6 tablespoons ground *ancho chilli* paste (see page 37) or 6 tablespoons *mole* powder (see page 19–20) or 3 table-spoons chilli powder
1 large onion, charred and coarsely chopped (see page 43)	
2 tablespoons oil	
6 tablespoons tomato purée	¹/₂ teaspoon sugar
1 litre (1³/₄ pints) meat stock (see page 40)	

METHOD ■ Blend the garlic, cinnamon and onion to a paste. Heat the oil in a large saucepan and add the paste. Cook, stirring constantly, for about 5 minutes or until it starts to dry up. Add the remaining ingredients and simmer for about 20 minutes or until the sauce thickens.

Pasta de Chile Seco

DRIED CHILLI PASTE

Dried chillies add another dimension to Mexican cuisine. Several types are often combined to create lovely and unusual flavours. The most popular combination is *ancho, pasilla* and *mulato,* but try any combination you wish and create your own new flavour.

Because the growing season in Mexico is almost entirely dependent on rainfall, the natives sought ways to feed themselves throughout the winter months. Hence, they use much dehydrated food which they dry in the sun. This applies to beans, corn for *tortillas,* and a great variety of chillies, some of which are also smoked and called *chilpotles.* The most popular varieties are *ancho* (large, very dark red); *mulato* (large, almost black); *pasilla* (black, long and thin); *chilpotle* (small, light brown, smoked); *guajillo* (small, pointed, smooth, dark red); *cascabel* (small, round, smooth, dark red); *chile de arbol* (similar to *guajillo* but thinner). There are many more but they are less popular.

METHOD ■ Dried chillies are very rich in vitamins and the hotness is very definitely concentrated in the seeds. They have to be washed, grilled for about 4 minutes, turning frequently, deseeded and stems removed, then soaked in hot water, milk or beer for about 1 hour. Reserve the seeds in case you wish to make the dish hotter later, or indeed for any other hot dish. Blend the chillies with their soaking liquid to a very smooth paste, and sieve it. The paste is now ready to be cooked as required in your recipe.

Salsa de Chile Chilpotle

SMOKED *JALAPEÑO* SAUCE

MAKES 600 ml
(1 pint)

Smoked *jalapeños* or *chilpotles*, as they are known in Mexico, are a delicacy. Combined with a basic tomato sauce you can use them on steak, *tacos*, or any type of cooked meat. Their smoky flavour is very popular.

INGREDIENTS

4 chipotle chillies or 100 g (4 oz) can of chilpotles	1 teaspoon oil
1 clove garlic, charred (see page 43)	¹/₂ quantity *Salsa para Enchiladas* (see page 35)
150 ml (¹/₄ pint) water or stock	

METHOD

■ If you are using canned *chilpotles*, blend the *Salsa para Enchiladas* with half the contents of the can and your *salsa* is ready to use.

■ If you are using dried *chilpotles*, treat them as recommended on page 37, and blend them with the garlic and water or stock. Heat the oil in a frying pan and fry the mixture for about 5 minutes. Add the *enchilada* sauce and simmer for a few minutes. The sauce is ready to use on meats or *antojitos*.

Salsa Borracha

TIPSY SAUCE

MAKES about
300 ml (¹/₂ pint)

Traditionally, this sauce is served with steamed lamb which we call *barbacoa*. It goes well with other meats and vegetables and *antojitos*, in much the same manner as *Salsa Típica*. Its name is derived from the addition of *pulque*, beer or tequila instead of stock or water. This recipe can be used with any other variety of dried chilli or a combination of chillies.

INGREDIENTS

10 cascabel or other dried chillies	¹/₂ onion, charred and coarsely chopped (see page 43)
150 ml (¹/₄ pint) pulque, beer or tequila	
2 ripe tomatoes, charred and peeled (see page 43)	¹/₂ teaspoon salt
	pinch of sugar
1 clove garlic, charred (see page 43)	1 tablespoon oil

METHOD

■ Prepare the chillies as described on page 37, but soak in hot beer instead of water. Blend to a purée with all the remaining ingredients, except the oil. Heat the oil in a frying pan, add the mixture, and fry for about 5 minutes, stirring occasionally. This sauce can be served hot or cold.

Caldo

STOCK

ᐯᐱᐯᐱ

MAKES 1 litre (1³/₄ pints)

Home-made soup is the most popular starter for Mexican meals, even when the midday sun is beating down! This is not surprising, since thrifty cooks look for ways of using the stock from boiled meats and chickens. It provides good, light nourishment and it costs very little.

Whether or not you are boiling meat or chicken, you can always make good stock with trimmings from roast beef or chicken carcasses, leftover gravy and vegetable peelings. A good stock could be the reason behind your success as a cook! This stock can be used for soups, meats, gravies, rice, pasta or *salsas*.

INGREDIENTS

1.5 kg (3¹/₂ lb) chicken and giblets (or other meats and bones)	6 sticks celery (including leaves), halved
2.3 litres (4 pints) water	3 carrots, unpeeled
1 teaspoon salt	6 cabbage leaves
¹/₂ teaspoon ground black pepper	2 turnips, unpeeled
3 tablespoons vinegar	3 cloves garlic
	3 large onions, halved or quartered

METHOD

■ Wash the chicken well and remove any small feathers, loose skin, etc. Wash the giblets, remove any yellow skin and check that the chicken liver has no green staining on it. If it has discard it altogether. Wash the chicken neck and put in a very large saucepan with the chicken and all the other ingredients. Bring to the boil and skim off any foam that rises to the surface. Cover, reduce the heat and simmer for at least 1 hour, then test for readiness by pricking a drumstick with a fork. If only clear liquid shows and the drumstick moves easily, remove the chicken. If the chicken is to be shredded, do it while it is still warm as the meat separates more easily from the skin and bones. The same applies to boiled meat.

■ Increase the heat and boil the stock rapidly for a further 20 minutes, uncovered, to reduce it. Strain and cool. If possible, refrigerate the stock as this will cause the fat to congeal on the top. Before use, remove the fat and strain the stock again.

NOTE If only bones or carcasses are being used for the stock, it is advisable to double the simmering time.

Pasta de Hojaldra Para Empanaditas

ROUGH PUFF PASTRY FOR *EMPANADITAS*

ᴧᴧᴧ

SERVES 6

*P*asta de hojaldra is more commonly used in Mexico than any other pastry. Its lightness provides mouthwatering results. Being economical with time, I have opted for this version. It is a rough puff pastry which is also very light and much quicker and easier to prepare.

INGREDIENTS

175 g (6 oz) self-raising flour	juice of ¹/₂ lemon
pinch of salt	75 ml (3 fl oz) cold water
50 g (2 oz) margarine, cubed	beaten egg yolk or milk, to glaze
50 g (2 oz) lard or white vegetable fat	Filling of your choice

METHOD

■ Sift the flour and salt together into a bowl, and toss in the fats, coating them with flour. Using two knives or a spatula, mix the lemon juice and water into the flour mixture without breaking the lumps of fat. Now add just enough extra liquid to bind the ingredients into a soft dough.

■ With floured fingers, gather the dough into a soft ball, place it on a well-floured board and shape it into a rectangle about 2.5 cm (1 inch) thick. Lightly mark the dough with two horizontal lines, dividing it into thirds. Fold the lower third towards the centre, trapping as much air as possible, and seal the edges together by pressing them with the rolling pin.

■ Fold the top half towards the centre and seal again. Repeat the rolling and folding process three times, turning the dough a quarter turn each time, then wrap the dough in cling film and refrigerate for at least 1 hour. Meanwhile, prepare and cool the filling which can be sweet or savoury.

■ Heat the oven to 220°C, 425°F, Gas Mark 7. Roll the pastry to the thickness of a coin and cut into circles. (A 15 cm/6 inch saucer is the right size for main course *empanadas* and a 5 cm/2 inch biscuit cutter will make 36 cocktail-sized ones.)

■ Place about 2 tablespoons filling in the centre of a 15 cm (6 inch) round (or a smaller amount, according to the size of the pastry). Dampen the edges of the dough with water, fold over and press together. Place on a baking tray, brush with egg or milk and prick once with a fork. Bake for about 15 minutes or until golden. Cool on a wire rack for a few minutes, then serve.

Methodos Para Pelar Chiles Poblanos

METHODS FOR PEELING FRESH GREEN CHILLIES

The most popular chillies used for stuffing are *poblanos*, but the green *pasilla* or *mulato* or the green capsicum (sweet pepper) may be used instead. They all have a relatively tough skin which, following the traditional ways of Mexican cooking, should be removed. In modern times, this is considered unnecessary as peppers are eaten raw in salads, skin and all. However, it is not only that Mexicans prefer chillies or peppers without the skin; certain steps, which involve removing the skin, are required to part-cook the chillies or peppers and intensify their flavour. Choose the method below that suits you best.

Grilling or Charring

Place the peppers under a hot grill and watch them blister. With cooking tongs, turn them as required, ensuring that most of the skin is scorched. As they are ready, place them in a strong polythene bag and leave them for 15 minutes before peeling.

Charring with Direct Heat

Place the peppers on a very hot griddle or heavy-based frying pan, and turn them as above until most of the skin is blistered or scorched. As they are ready, place them in a strong plastic bag and leave them for 15 minutes before peeling.

Frying

Fry the peppers in hot oil in a deep-fryer until blisters appear on all sides. The oil might splatter and cause burns so be extra careful with this procedure. Remove them from the oil and wrap them in kitchen paper towels. Place them in a strong polythene bag and leave them for 15 minutes before peeling.

Peeling and Destalking

Leaving the charred chillies or peppers wrapped in a polythene bag enhances their flavour while they cook further. It also allows the skins to be removed easily. In Mexico, if we are going to stuff the chillies or peppers we leave the stalks on and cut a slit in the side to remove the seeds; in England I hesitate to do this because people feel compelled to eat the stalk! I leave it to your discretion whether you wish to remove the stalks or not. If you do, then stuff the chillies or peppers from the top after you have removed the seeds and stalk.

Freezing

Scorched, grilled or fried peppers freeze very well, peeled or unpeeled. Wrap them individually before freezing; the skin comes off quite easily when thawed.

Charred Vegetables

Charring onions, garlic, tomatoes and peppers before skinning gives them a lovely sweet, smoky flavour and a juicy texture. This method is very popular in Mexico where vegetables are charred on a hot griddle. In England, they can be charred under the grill or in a hot heavy-based frying pan, and turned frequently until black and blistered. Peel when cool enough to handle.

Sazon Para Carnes, Aves y Pescados

MEAT, POULTRY AND FISH SEASONING

MAKES enough for 450 g (1 lb) meat, poultry or fish

Seasoning your food carefully always pays dividends. The flavour is never as good when salt and pepper are added at the last minute. The acidity of vinegar or lemon juice enhances stocks, soups and gravies in a similar way that wine does; it preserves meats and fish and it also tenderises. I usually use vinegar for any type of meat or poultry and lemon for fish and shellfish.

Being able to measure the seasoning by the weight of the meat helps. The quantities indicated below are calculated for boneless meats. If you are roasting a turkey, you would have to weigh it and deduct from the total weight before you determine the amount of seasoning. (As a rule of thumb, the carcass will weigh about half the total weight of the bird.) Remember that you can always add more seasoning halfway through cooking but you cannot take excessive seasoning away.

INGREDIENTS

1 tablespoon malt vinegar or lemon juice	1 clove garlic, charred and crushed (see page 43)
1/4 teaspoon salt	1/2 onion, charred and roughly chopped (see page 43)
1/4 teaspoon ground black pepper	
pinch of sugar	

METHOD

■ Mix the vinegar, salt, pepper and sugar together, and brush it over the prepared meat or fish. Rub the meat or fish with the garlic and onion, and leave to marinate for at least 1 hour. The meat or fish can now be roasted, baked, poached, simmered, grilled or barbecued, and the stock or gravy will be well flavoured.

VARIATION

Steak seasoned and marinated in beer instead of vinegar is absolutely delicious.

ANTOJITOS

▲▲▲▲▲▲▲▲▲▲▲▲▲▲▲▲

ANTOJITOS (little whims or 'what you fancy') are meant to attract your attention and make your mouth water – similar to the Spanish *tapas*, they aim to satisfy your appetite whether you are hungry or not! The word *antojito* covers a whole range of Mexican food, from fruit peeled and cut to look like a flower, then sprinkled with lime juice, salt and cayenne, to *tacos*, *tamales*, *enchiladas*, *tortas* or *quesadillas*.

In Mexico, *antojitos* are cooked anywhere and everywhere; you can buy them on street corners, outside cinemas, at schools, on the roadside, in homes, restaurants, markets, parks or at bullfights. Eating in the street is quite common, and you will often see groups of people drinking beer and eating *antojitos* as you walk down the street.

Since mealtimes are not set in Mexico, *antojitos* are hard to resist. At Mexican markets you will see women with freshly made *tortillas* offering *barbacoa* with a chilli sauce, next to the fellow who, armed with an orange squeezer, has put up a stall selling freshly squeezed orange juice by the pint. In the evening, after the theatre, you have to be very strong to walk straight past the corner stall offering freshly made *quesadillas* filled with pumpkin blossoms and a little cheese.

Any of the recipes in this chapter fall within the *antojitos* category. They can be served as starters, if you make them small, or as main courses, if you make them larger.

Pepitas

ROASTED PUMPKIN SEEDS

SERVES 4

Pepitas are so common in Mexico that you learn to eat them very early in childhood. Indian women sit on the floor with a small clean cloth in front of them and on it are small piles of roasted and salted *pepitas*. The price is a few *centavos* and children love cracking the very brittle shells and getting at the seed. They are often used in main dishes, but I prefer them just as an aperitif. You can buy them shelled at health food stores or Chinese supermarkets.

INGREDIENTS

150 g (5 oz) shelled pumpkin seeds	¹/₄ teaspoon salt

METHOD

■ Heat a heavy-based frying pan and place the pumpkin seeds in it. Stir continually over medium heat until the seeds start to pop. Cover, shake and return to the heat. Cook for about a further 1 minute, shaking frequently, until the shells puff up and brown a little. Add the salt, cover and shake once more. Serve cold.

Totopos

CORN *TORTILLA* CHIPS

SERVES 4

Totopos, or *tortilla* chips as they are now known in the UK, are seldom sold commercially in Mexico, because it is a good way of using up stale *tortillas*, and every home in Mexico has an adequate supply. *Totopos* are ideal for dips; they are stronger than potato crisps and cheaper than biscuits. They can be flavoured with salt, cayenne or Parmesan cheese – or all three. *Totopos* can be made from wheat or corn *tortillas*, but those made from wheat are much more brittle and I would not recommend using them for dips. Serve with drinks and *guacamole*.

INGREDIENTS

oil for deep-frying	2 tablespoons freshly grated Parmesan cheese (optional)
12 corn *tortillas* (see page 24), each cut into six	1 teaspoon cayenne pepper
1¹/₂ teaspoons salt	

METHOD

■ Heat the oil in a deep-fryer to 180°C, 350°F. Place half the *tortilla* pieces in the frying basket and carefully lower it into the hot oil, lifting it out for a moment if the bubbling becomes too fierce. Fry the chips for about 3 minutes or until golden brown and crisp, shaking the basket frequently. Remove and drain the chips on absorbent kitchen paper. Repeat the process with the remaining *tortillas*. While still hot, sprinkle with salt, cheese and/or cayenne. Serve cold.

■ To store, place the cold chips in an airtight container and keep for up to 1 week. If they lose their crispness, just place them in a hot oven for 5 minutes.

Nachos

TORTILLA CHIPS WITH MELTED CHEESE

SERVES 6

*N*achos are an American idea, but they retain a Mexican identity. They are easy to make at home, with little last-minute preparation required – you just pop them into the oven as your guests arrive. Serve hot with drinks.

INGREDIENTS

oil for deep-frying	100 g (4 oz) mozzarella cheese, coarsely grated
12 corn *tortillas* (see page 24), cut into quarters	4 bottled or canned *jalapeño* chillies, sliced, or 4 fresh chillies, sliced
225 g (8 oz) Cheddar cheese, coarsely grated	

METHOD

■ Heat the oil in a deep-fryer to 180°C, 350°F. Place half the *tortilla* pieces in the frying basket and carefully lower it into the hot oil, lifting it out for a moment if the bubbling becomes too fierce. Shaking the basket, fry the chips for about 3 minutes or until golden brown and crisp. Remove and drain on absorbent kitchen paper. Repeat the process with the remaining *tortillas*.

■ Spread the chips on baking trays and sprinkle them individually with the grated cheeses and chillies. Bake in the oven at 220°C, 425°F, Gas Mark 7 for 8 minutes or until the cheese melts. Serve immediately.

Guacamole

AVOCADO DIP

SERVES 6;
makes about
600 ml (1 pint)

I believe *guacamole* to be the most popular of Mexican dishes. It makes an excellent hors d'oeuvre served with *totopos* and drinks, an attractive garnish, a delicious filling for *fajitas* and soft *tacos*, or a side dish to accompany any other Mexican *antojito*, rice, meat or salad. *Guacamole* is an Aztec word: *guaca* means pear-shaped and *mole* means sauce.

INGREDIENTS

3 firm, ripe tomatoes, finely chopped	juice of ¹/₂ lime or lemon
6 sprigs fresh coriander, finely chopped	³/₄ teaspoon salt
¹/₂ onion or 4 spring onions, finely chopped	¹/₂ teaspoon ground black pepper
2 green chillies, finely chopped	2 medium-sized ripe avocados

METHOD

■ Mix together all the ingredients, except the avocados, not more than 2 hours before serving. Cover with cling film until required. This will draw the juices from the onions and tomatoes, and thus provide the liquid required to make the *guacamole* creamy.

■ About 30 minutes before serving, cut the avocados in half, remove and reserve the stones, and spoon out the flesh, scraping the skins clean. Mash with a fork and mix into the vegetable mixture. Serve in a shallow bowl, placing an avocado stone in the centre of the dish to prevent the *guacamole* discolouring. Cover with cling film until required. Just before serving, place the bowl on a small tray and surround with *totopos*.

OPPOSITE   Clockwise from top: *Frijoles Refritos* (re-fried beans, page 31), *Enchiladas Suizas* (tortillas stuffed with chicken, cream and cheese, page 66), *Totopos* (homemade tortilla chips, page 46) and *Ensalada Tenango* (avocado and tomato salad, page 175)

Chilaquiles

TORTILLA CHIPS IN TOMATO SAUCE

SERVES 4

Chilaquiles is a popular dish all over Mexico. It is usually served for *almuerzo* (brunch) or for a light supper. It is the Mexican equivalent to Italian pasta and just as tasty as you wish to make it. I use it often because it is versatile and quick to prepare, especially if you already have some of the crispy salted *tortilla* chips now available in supermarkets.

INGREDIENTS

oil for deep-frying	¹/₄ teaspoon sugar
10 corn *tortillas* (see page 24), each cut into eight pieces, or 225 g (8 oz) salted *tortilla* chips	¹/₂ teaspoon salt (if salted *tortilla* chips are not used)
1 tablespoon oil	300 ml (¹/₂ pint) water
1 onion, finely chopped	GARNISH
2 tablespoons tomato purée	¹/₂ onion, very finely chopped
1 chicken stock cube	4 tablespoons soured cream
2 green chillies	100 g (4 oz) *queso fresco* or white Cheshire cheese, crumbled
¹/₄ teaspoon ground black pepper	

METHOD

■ Heat the oil in a deep-fryer to 180°C, 350°F. Fry the *tortilla* pieces in two batches for about 3 minutes each or until they just change colour. Drain on absorbent kitchen paper and keep warm.

■ Heat 1 tablespoon oil in a frying pan and fry the onion for 2 minutes or until golden. Add the tomato purée, stock cube, whole chillies, black pepper, sugar, salt and water, and simmer for 15 minutes over medium heat or until the sauce thickens and reduces by about half. Remove the chillies or chop them and return them to the sauce if you want the dish to be hot.

■ Just before serving, toss the *tortilla* chips in the sauce, making sure they are well covered. Place them on a serving dish and top with chopped onion, soured cream and crumbled cheese.

OPPOSITE   Clockwise from top: *Caldo Tlalpeño* (chicken soup with avocado slices, page 83), *Quesadillas Sonorenses* (wheat flour tortillas filled with cheese, page 59) and *Sopa de Frijol Negro* (black bean soup, page 85)

Uchepos

FRESH MAIZE *TAMALES*

SERVES 4;
makes 12 small
uchepos

This dish is a favourite for breakfast. Light and easy to prepare, it can be used as a side dish for any Mexican meal. I have eaten them with scrambled eggs and black beans. You may generally use them instead of bread. Use sugar instead of salt if you prefer them sweet. Because fresh corn is not available all the time, frozen sweetcorn can be used instead, thawed out the night before and left uncovered overnight to allow excess moisture to evaporate. Use waxed (not greaseproof) paper instead of the green leaves, if necessary. Flavour-wise, you miss a little and I must say the light spring green of the natural leaves looks very appetising and adds a little something extra to the dish.

INGREDIENTS

12 large fresh corn cobs or 1 kg (2 lb)
   frozen sweetcorn, thawed

pinch of salt or 1 teaspoon sugar

24 fresh green corn husks or twelve 20 cm
   (8 inch) squares of waxed paper

2 *chiles poblanos* or green peppers,
   charred, peeled and deseeded
   (see page 42)

1 teaspoon oil

2 green chillies, finely chopped

100 g (4 oz) soured cream

cayenne pepper, to garnish

METHOD

■ To remove the leaves from fresh corn cobs, carefully peel them back towards the base, revealing the kernels. Insert a sharp knife at the base to pull the cob away without disturbing the leaves any further (they tend to split lengthways easily). Wash the leaves in hot water and drain.

■ Cut the kernels from the cobs as near to the core as possible. Put in a blender or food processor and blend to a rough-textured purée. Mix in the salt (or sugar), working quickly to avoid the mixture turning bitter. Place a wide leaf or square of waxed paper in the palm of your hand and put one heaped tablespoon of the mixture in it. Fold two opposite sides of the leaf or paper over the filling, overlapping the edges, and fold the leaf tip or the other two sides of the paper underneath to make a neat parcel. Place it in the top of a steamer and repeat to make eleven more *uchepos*. Cover with more leaves or brown paper. Put the lid on and steam for 40 minutes or until the mixture separates easily from the leaf.

■ Cut the peppers into long strips. Heat the oil in a frying pan and sauté the peppers and chillies until soft. Add the soured cream and heat through without boiling. Transfer to a dish and garnish with a sprinkling of cayenne. Serve the peppers separately, to be spooned over the unwrapped *uchepos*.

Empanaditas de Picadillo

—— TURNOVERS WITH MINCED BEEF, ALMONDS AND OLIVES ——

SERVES 4;
makes 8
empanaditas

It is very likely that *empanadas* were introduced into Mexico by the Cornish miners who came to work in the gold, silver and copper mines. As other foreign dishes, they were adopted and adapted to the Mexican palate and way of cooking. They are light, delicious and excellent as a starter with drinks. Larger *empanadas* are popular served as a main course with vegetables in a similar manner to Cornish pasties.

Picadillo is the most popular way of eating minced beef in Mexico. This recipe is also used to stuff *chiles rellenos* and *chiles en nogada,* or served with rice and warm *tortillas* as a main course.

INGREDIENTS

PICADILLO	1 green chilli, chopped
100 g (4 oz) minced beef	1 red pepper, deseeded and sliced
100 g (4 oz) minced pork	3 sticks celery, finely chopped
2 teaspoons vinegar	1 small potato, cooked, peeled and cubed
$\frac{1}{4}$ teaspoon salt	9 stuffed olives, sliced
$\frac{1}{4}$ teaspoon ground black pepper	1 teaspoon flaked almonds
$\frac{1}{4}$ teaspoon sugar	1 tablespoon raisins
1 tablespoon oil	400 g (14 oz) can peeled tomatoes, crushed
$\frac{1}{2}$ onion, charred and finely chopped (see page 43)	1 tablespoon tomato purée
1 clove garlic, charred and crushed (see page 43)	1 quantity Rough Puff Pastry (see page 41)

METHOD

■ Mix the meats and season with the vinegar, salt, pepper and sugar. Heat the oil in a frying pan, and fry the onion, garlic, chilli, red pepper and celery for 3 minutes. Add the meat and stir over high heat for about 10 minutes or until it starts to brown. (This sometimes takes longer than you would expect if the vegetables have a high water content, so just continue frying until the liquid is absorbed.) Discard any surplus oil, taking care to retain the meat juices. Add the remaining ingredients, except the pastry, and simmer for 15 minutes or until the mixture starts to dry out, stirring occasionally. Allow to cool. Use the puff pastry and fill and bake as described on page 41.

Corundas

STEAMED TRIANGULAR CORN DUMPLINGS

SERVES 6

Corundas could be called poor man's fare. They are used instead of bread to mop up sauces or gravy from stews or beans, rather like dumplings in England, but they are also often eaten as a snack with sauce and cheese. *Corundas* are traditionally steamed wrapped in the long and narrow leaf of the maize plant (rather than the husk from the corn cob like *tamales*). Their finished shape is usually triangular due to the way the leaf has to be folded in order to wrap the dough. They refrigerate very well and freeze well too. They are very bland and if you are a vegetarian, I suggest you use butter or vegetable margarine instead of lard. Waxed (not greaseproof) paper strips can be used if leaves are not available.

INGREDIENTS

12 fresh green maize plant leaves or twenty 8 x 25 cm (3 x 10 inch) strips of waxed paper

2 litres (4 pints) boiling water

275 g (10 oz) *masa harina* (see page 19)

600 ml (18 fl oz) warm milk

75 g (3 oz) lard or butter, softened

1 tablespoon baking powder

¼ teaspoon salt

GARNISH

1 *Salsa para Enchilada* (see page 35)

100 g (4 oz) curd cheese

METHOD

■ Wash the leaves and immerse them in the boiling water. Cover and leave until you are ready to use them. If you are using waxed paper, cut the pieces and have them ready. Place the *masa harina* in a warm bowl and gradually add the milk alternately with the lard. Add the baking powder and salt, and beat with an electric mixer until bubbles appear. The consistency should be that of very thick porridge. To test the dough for readiness, drop a little into a tumbler of cold water; it should float and stick together. If it has not been beaten enough it will separate.

■ Drain the leaves in a colander. Take a leaf or piece of waxed paper and fold it diagonally along the middle (see **1** opposite). Then fold the left hand part of the strip across to the right (**2**). Turn it round and drop a tablespoon of dough into the triangular cavity (**3** and **4**). Fold the top of the leaf or paper over (**5**) and flatten slightly. Fold the edges round the triangular shape (**6**). Line the top of a steamer with maize leaves or brown paper and place the *corundas* flat in the bottom and around the sides. Cover with several layers of leaves or brown paper. Cover tightly and steam for about 2 hours, adding more water to the bottom of the pan if necessary. To serve, remove the leaves or waxed papers and cover the *corundas* with hot *Salsa* and curd cheese, or serve them with *frijoles de olla*, *mole* or any saucy stew.

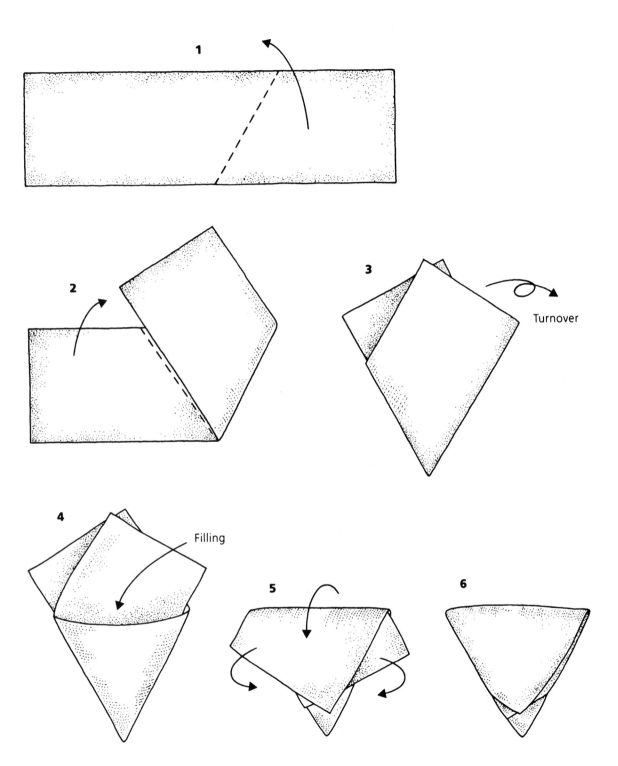

1

2

3

Turnover

4

Filling

5

6

Tamales

CORN DUMPLINGS WITH MEAT AND SAUCE

MAKES 30

*T*amales consist mainly of maize dough with a little meat and some sauce; they are usually wrapped in either banana leaves in the south of Mexico or in corn husks in the rest of the country. Anything wrapped in this manner and steamed is also called *tamal* so it can be a little confusing; if you ask for a *tamal de Pescado* at a restaurant, you will get steamed fish, nicely seasoned and with a sauce all cooked inside a leaf but without any corn dough.

Tamales are amongst the oldest of Mexican dishes – they were served at Aztec banquets. They are so popular in Mexico today that there are shops which sell nothing but *tamales*. They can be filled with every conceivable vegetable, meat and sauce, or simply prepared on their own without flavouring to eat with a sauce, straight from the corn husks.

Since *tamales* are time-consuming to prepare, I make a large amount and freeze them in their husks. This recipe makes about 30, so you could make 10 red, 10 green and 10 sweet *tamales*. It is easy to tell the difference between the red and green ones, because the red stains the husks while the green ones appear to stay clean. Freshly made *tamales* can be kept in the refrigerator for up to 3 days and reheated by steaming for 10–15 minutes; microwaving for 2 minutes or by shallow-frying – but I warn you, your waist will suffer!

If you can't get corn husks, use 20 cm (8 inch) squares of kitchen foil with waxed (not greaseproof) paper squares placed on top. For the savoury filling you can use pork, beef, chicken, turkey or fish, *frijoles*, *rajas*, cheese or a combination of your liking.

INGREDIENTS

60 or more corn husks or 20 cm (8 inch) squares of kitchen foil and waxed paper (see above)

TAMAL DOUGH

750 g (1½ lb) *masa harina* (see page 19)

1.3 litres (2¼ pints) warm stock

225 g (8 oz) lard, softened

4 tablespoons baking powder

1 teaspoon salt

SAVOURY FILLING FOR 10 RED AND 10 GREEN *TAMALES*

750 g (1½ lb) cooked meat, coarsely shredded

1½ quantities *Salsa Adobada* (see page 36)

1½ quantities *Salsa de Tomate Verde* (see page 33)

FILLING FOR 10 SWEET *TAMALES*

3 tablespoons sugar

2 drops cochineal

10 glacé cherries, chopped

4 slices crystallised pineapple, chopped

2 tablespoons raisins

METHOD

■ Soak the corn husks overnight to soften them. (Alternatively, cover them completely with water, bring them to the boil and drain.) In a large bowl, mix together the *masa harina*, lukewarm stock and softened lard. Add the baking powder, and beat until bubbles start to appear. To test the dough for readiness, drop a little into a glass of cold water – it should float and stick together. If it drops to the bottom and disintegrates, keep on mixing. You should have a warm, sloppy dough similar to a cake mixture. If you are making sweet *tamales*, separate one-third of the dough before adding the salt.

■ Overlap two corn husks lengthways in the palm of one hand and spoon in 1 tablespoon sauce, 1 tablespoon dough and some cooked meat. Finally, add another 1 tablespoon sauce. Wrap the husks carefully around the filling, overlapping the edges, then fold the tail end towards the top, leaving it loose to allow room for expansion. If using waxed paper and kitchen foil, place the dough, sauce and meat in the centre, then wrap loosely, allowing for expansion. Pinch the ends of the foil to make it watertight.

■ To make sweet *tamales*, stir in the sugar and cochineal instead of the salt. Replace the meat and sauce filling with the mixed fruits. Dab the husks with a little cochineal to distinguish them from the savoury *tamales* then arrange all the *tamales* in the top half of a steamer and cover with greaseproof paper. Cover tightly and steam for $1^1/_2$ hours, topping up with hot water when necessary.

■ To test when done, carefully open one or two *tamales* and pinch the dough between your fingers. It should be light and fluffy. If it feels sticky, cook for a little longer. Heat any leftover sauces separately and place them on the table for people to add a little to each *tamal* if they wish.

Tamal de Cazuela

CORN DOUGH SAVOURY CASSEROLE

When corn husks are not available, or you are in a hurry, this recipe is a good substitute for *tamales* at half the preparation time. Although not so authentic, the dish is just as flavourful. Use the recipe for *tamales*, but instead of wrapping the dough, filling and sauce in corn husks, assemble them in the following way:

METHOD

- Grease two 20 x 30 cm (8 x 12 inch) ovenproof dishes. Generously cover the bottom of each dish with *salsa*, then spoon some of the dough on to it to resemble small islands, leaving room for them to expand during cooking. Place large pieces of cooked meat on top, then cover with more sauce. Layer the rest of the dough, meat and sauce in the same way, reserving a little of the sauce. Cover very tightly with foil and bake in the centre of the oven at 180°C, 350°F, Gas Mark 4 for about 1 hour. Prick the dough with a fork to test for readiness. Heat the reserved sauce and serve with the *tamal*.

- For cocktail parties, I make *Tamal de Cazuela*, cut it into 2.5 cm (1 inch) squares, place it in paper cake cases, and serve it hot.

Tamales Oaxaqueños

MAIZE DUMPLINGS STEAMED IN BANANA LEAVES

MAKES 18

In the South Pacific region of Mexico, with its tropical climate, cooking in banana leaves is customary. In Britain, there are a few places where you might be able to get banana leaves, such as in Soho, where some of the Oriental merchants receive their exotic fruits wrapped in them. If you can find them, the chances are you can buy them for a pittance. If they are unobtainable, the alternative is pieces of waxed (not greaseproof) paper and kitchen foil squares, about 25 cm (10 inches) square. Unlike the corn *tamales* that finish up in a sort of rounded, long, fat, sausage-roll shape, Oaxaca's *tamales* are usually flat and rectangular.

The steaming is done in a similar manner to other *tamales*, and the leaves have to be plunged into boiling water to soften them before use. This recipe calls for *mole negro*, made from a special variety of chilli called *chilhuacle*, which is burned to a cinder. This colours the dough and gives it a distinct flavour. If *mole negro* is unobtainable, double the amount of *mulato* chilli used. Should all Mexican chillies be unobtainable, use 4 tablespoons ground dried chillies. These *tamales* can be prepared in advance: preparation time is about 4 hours. They freeze well and microwave too.

INGREDIENTS

4 *ancho* chillies	750 g (1¼ lb) canned tomatoes, mashed
4 *mulato* chillies	175 g (6 oz) *mole negro de Oaxaca* or 4 tablespoons ground dried chillies
1 litre (2 pints) hot chicken stock	
4 cloves garlic	about 4 pieces banana leaves or eighteen 25 cm (10 inch) waxed paper and kitchen foil squares
1 large onion, quartered	
½ teaspoon dried oregano	
2 chicken stock cubes	1.8 kg (4 lb) chicken, boiled
¼ teaspoon ground black pepper	1 quantity *tamal* dough (see page 54)
1 tablespoon oil	

METHOD

■ Heat the chillies in a hot dry frying pan for 3 minutes. Remove and discard the stems and seeds, then soak in 300 ml (½ pint) of the stock for 30 minutes or until soft. Put the chillies and their liquid in a blender with the garlic, onion, oregano, chicken stock cubes and pepper, and blend to a smooth paste. Heat the oil in a large saucepan and sieve the mixture into it. Fry for 5 minutes, stirring, then add the tomatoes, *mole negro* or chilli powder and remaining stock. Simmer for 20 minutes or until the sauce thickens. If you have managed to obtain banana leaves, remove and discard the centre stalks. To soften the leaves, plunge them into boiling water for 10 minutes. Drain and pat dry.

■ Skin, bone and shred the cooked chicken. Strain the dough mixture to ensure it is very smooth and makes a very fine textured *tamal*. Place 2 table-spoons dough in the centre of a 25 cm (10 inch) square of leaf or kitchen foil lined with waxed paper. Press down to about 1 cm (½ inch) thickness. Follow with a piece of meat and enough sauce to cover the surface of the dough. Overlap the sides and ends of the dough to form square parcels. Secure with cotton, string or a strip of banana leaf. (Kitchen foil parcels will not need securing in this manner; folding is sufficient.) Arrange the parcels in the top half of a steamer and cover with a few banana leaves or grease-proof paper. Cover tightly and steam for 1½ hours, topping up with hot water when necessary. These *tamales* can be kept in the refrigerator for 3 days or frozen in their leaves. Serve hot, uncovering the *tamal*, but keeping the leaf as decoration around it by folding the sides back. Do not eat the leaf!

Queso Fundido or Chili Con Queso

MELTED CHEESE WITH CHILLI AND *CHORIZO*

SERVES 6

Queso Fundido is a Mexican version of fondue, except you do not make your own at the table. In restaurants, they put the cheese in pretty clay pots together with the rest of the ingredients and then bring it to the table with warm corn or wheat flour *tortillas*. The most commonly used cheese in the north is *queso asadero*; in the South Pacific region *queso de Oaxaca* is popular, and in the rest of the country any good melting cheese. The *Salsa de Jitomate Típica* and the *tortillas* enhance the dish and give it its Mexican flavour.

INGREDIENTS

1 teaspoon oil	200 g (7 oz) *queso asadero* or mild Cheddar cheese, grated
200 g (7 oz) *chorizo* (see page 18)	
¹/₂ onion, thinly sliced	200 g (7 oz) *queso de oaxaca, queso pera* or mozzarella, grated
4 green chillies, cut into strips	

METHOD

■ Heat the oil in a heavy-based saucepan and fry the chorizo until very crispy. Add the onion and chillies, and continue frying for 4 minutes. Drain, then divide among six ramekin dishes or small ovenproof clay pots of a similar size. Put equal amounts of each cheese in the ramekins and bake in the oven at 180°C, 350°F, Gas Mark 4 for about 15 minutes or until the cheese just melts and starts to bubble. Serve immediately with warm *tortillas* and *Salsa de Jitomate Típica* (page 34).

Quesadillas Mexicanas

CORN *TORTILLAS* WITH MELTED CHEESE

SERVES 4

Mexicans enjoy eating in the open air and *quesadillas* are a favourite. Street vendors make them in the traditional way, filling uncooked *tortillas* and then shallow-frying them to create an irresistible aroma for passers-by. This recipe has been adjusted to use ready-cooked *tortillas*, which are much more convenient and can be eaten as a snack or a light lunch or supper.

INGREDIENTS	8 cooked corn *tortillas* (see page 24)	200 g (70 oz) cheese (any type), sliced or grated

METHOD

■ Warm the *tortillas* on a hot griddle or in a hot, heavy-based frying pan, for about 30 seconds. Place some cheese on one half of the warm *tortilla* and fold over the other half to cover the cheese, pressing it down for a few seconds with a fish slice. Proceed with the rest in the same manner, turning each *quesadilla* as the cheese starts to melt and the *tortilla* gets slightly crisp. Serve immediately garnished with any kind of *salsa*.

Quesadillas Sonorenses

—— WHEAT FLOUR *TORTILLAS* FILLED WITH CHEESE ——

SERVES 4

Famous for its beautiful women, Sonora is also famous for its wheat flour *tortillas* filled with cheese.

INGREDIENTS	six 15 cm (6 inch) wheat flour *tortillas* (see page 26)	4 bottled or canned *jalapeños*, cut into strips
	175 g (6 oz) Cheddar cheese, coarsely grated	¹/₂ onion, sliced

METHOD

■ Cover half of each *tortilla* with cheese, a few strips of chilli and some onion rings. Fold the other half over and place on a hot griddle that has been lightly brushed with oil. When the cheese starts to melt, turn the *tortilla* over. Remove from the heat when the cheese is fully melted. Drain on absorbent kitchen paper and keep warm until all the *tortillas* are ready. Cut each *tortilla* into six triangles and garnish them individually with *salsa* or *guacamole*.

Quesadillas de Flor de Calabaza

PUMPKIN BLOSSOM TURNOVERS IN MAIZE PASTRY

SERVES 4

Flores de calabaza are frequently used in Mexican dishes, soups and casseroles, but they are best known as a filling for *quesadillas*. They are fun to buy as the colourful bright yellow blossoms adorn the market stalls and make an attractive picture. They are quite acceptable canned. They taste delicious with lots of green chilli and tomato sauce.

My most vivid memory of these *quesadillas* is from the streets of Mexico at night, when vendors sit at street corners and make *quesadillas* by hand. They pit-a-pat the *tortillas*, stop to put the filling on one half, and then fold the other half over the filling, press and fry. It is the smell that makes them absolutely irresistible; you have to be very strong-willed to go past the queue without joining it.

INGREDIENTS

FILLING	DOUGH
350 g (12 oz) pumpkin blossoms	150 g (5 oz) *masa harina* (see page 19)
1 tablespoon oil	1 teaspoon baking powder
¹/₂ onion, finely chopped	1 teaspoon salt
2 green chillies, finely chopped	50 g (2 oz) plain flour
1 tablespoon tomato purée	1 tablespoon lard
¹/₄ teaspoon salt	2 tablespoons double cream
1 tablespoon water	150 ml (¹/₄ pint) warm water
pinch of ground black pepper	175 g (6 oz) lard or 175 ml (6 fl oz) oil for frying
1 tablespoon chopped fresh *epazote* or coriander	

METHOD

■ To prepare the filling, wash the pumpkin blossoms, then trim off and discard the stems and 'whiskers'. Heat the oil in a frying pan and sauté the onion until soft. Add the chopped blossoms and the rest of the ingredients and fry, stirring, for about 5 minutes. Cool.

■ To prepare the dough, mix together the dry ingredients. Rub in the lard, then stir in the cream and water. Knead for about 5 minutes to a soft dough. Press into *tortillas* as instructed for Corn *Tortillas* on page 24. When you take the first layer of waxed paper off the pressed *tortilla*, cover half the *tortilla* with a tablespoon of the filling, leaving about 1 cm (¹/₂ inch) around the edges. Fold the *tortilla* in half, without removing the waxed paper. Press the edges to seal.

■ Heat the lard or oil in a frying pan. Peel off the waxed paper from one side of the *tortilla* and very carefully lower the filled *tortilla* into the pan, keeping the waxed paper on top but removing it as soon as possible. (The process is similar to that of cooking *tortillas*, but care must be taken when dealing with hot fat.) Fry the *quesadillas*, one at a time, over moderate heat until golden on one side, then turn over. When golden, remove from the heat, drain on absorbent kitchen paper and keep in a warm place until all the *quesadillas* are ready. Eat immediately; they do not reheat successfully.

VARIATION

If you do not wish to fry the *quesadillas*, cook them on a hot griddle as if they were *tortillas*.

Quesadillas De San Luis

CHILLI *TORTILLA* WITH CHEESE

SERVES 4

These *quesadillas* take their name from San Luis Potosí, a northern state of Mexico where they grind *ancho* chillies and mix them into the maize dough. This has the effect of flavouring the dough and colouring it a dark reddish brown. When served with traditional *quesadillas*, alternating the plain with the coloured, the dish looks most attractive. It makes a good hors d'oeuvre or starter garnished with radishes and shredded lettuce. Preparation must start 2 hours before required.

INGREDIENTS

2 *ancho* chillies	25 g (1 oz) lard
150 ml (¼ pint) boiling water	2 tablespoons double cream
150 g (5 oz) *masa harina* (see page 19)	100 g (4 oz) Cheddar cheese, grated
1 teaspoon baking powder	2 green chillies, thinly sliced lengthways (optional)
1 teaspoon salt	oil for shallow-frying
50 g (2 oz) plain flour	

METHOD

■ Heat the *ancho* chillies in a dry heavy-based frying pan, turning them until they soften. Discard the seeds and stalks, then soak the chillies in the boiling water for 1 hour.

■ Meanwhile, mix together the dry ingredients, rub in the lard and stir in the cream. Put the chillies and their liquid in a blender and blend to a fine paste for about 1 minute at high speed. Mix with the *masa harina* mixture and knead for about 5 minutes to a soft dough. Press the dough into *tortillas* as instructed for corn *tortillas* (see page 24).

■ Take the first piece of waxed paper off each pressed *tortilla*, and cover half the *tortilla* with grated cheese and strips of green chillies, if using, leaving about 1 cm (½ inch) around the edges. Fold in half and seal the edges by lightly moistening them with cold water and pressing them together.

■ Pour enough oil into a frying pan to cover the bottom nicely and heat it. When the oil is hot, carefully lower a *tortilla* into it, removing the second piece of paper as you do so. Fry for about 3 minutes or until golden, turning once. Drain on absorbent kitchen paper. Repeat to cook the remaining *quesadillas*. Serve hot.

Quesadillas de Chorizo Y Papa

TORTILLAS WITH *CHORIZO* AND POTATO

SERVES 4

Quesadillas are an *antojito* of which there are innumerable variations. Like *tacos*, practically anything can go into a *quesadilla* because what makes it so palatable is the crispy maize wrapping. Therefore, leftover *mole* and spicy meat or vegetables of any kind can be turned into a delicious nibble. Mashed potato is very popular in *quesadillas*, despite the fact that it makes them slightly dry. Flavoured with a little chilli and *epazote* as well as cheese or *chorizo*, they are delicious.

INGREDIENTS

1 teaspoon cooking oil	150 g (5 oz) Cheddar cheese, grated
1/2 onion, finely chopped	8 cooked corn *tortillas* (see page 24) or dough recipe for *Quesadillas de Flor de Calabaza* (see page 60)
2 green chillies, thinly cut lengthways (optional)	
100 g (4 oz) *chorizo*, chopped	4 sprigs fresh *epazote* or coriander, chopped
225 g (8 oz) potatoes, boiled and mashed	
salt and ground black pepper	

METHOD

■ Heat the oil in a frying pan and fry the onion and chillies, if using, until soft. Add the *chorizo* and fry, stirring, until it is dark red and crispy. Add the potatoes and season with salt and pepper. Remove from the pan and stir in the grated cheese.

■ Heat the *tortillas* on a very hot griddle for about 30 seconds. Spoon some filling on half of each *tortilla* and add some *epazote* or coriander. Fold the other half of the *tortilla* over and secure with a cocktail stick. Repeat until all the *tortillas* have been filled.

■ Heat the griddle again until a few drops of water sizzle on it. Place a *quesadilla* on the griddle for 45 seconds, turn over and heat for a further 45 seconds or until both sides are done and the cheese is well melted. Repeat until all the *quesadillas* are heated. Serve immediately. If you prefer, the filled *quesadillas* can be shallow-fried.

Enchiladas Con Queso Y Cebolla

TORTILLAS STUFFED WITH CHEESE

SERVES 4

*E*nchiladas are *tortillas* filled, rolled and covered in a sauce. This is originally a vegetarian dish and it is served in Mexico by itself, with refried beans or as a side dish with grilled meats. *Enchiladas* are the most popular of the *tortilla* dishes – a well-deserved popularity, because they are an excellent combination of flavour, texture and colour. *Enchiladas* are more commonly prepared with corn *tortillas*, but wheat flour *tortillas* may also be treated in exactly the same way.

A good *salsa* is as important as a good *tortilla*. Traditionally, *enchiladas* have no meat; they are filled with chopped raw onion and crumbled cheese, then rolled up, with generous amounts of boiling sauce poured over them, followed by more onions and cheese for garnish. Beans are an excellent companion to this dish, garnished with very finely shredded lettuce.

The sauce may be of any type. Tomato-based sauces make the most well-known *enchiladas*, but you will find you can make them with any type of sauce with equally delicious results. If you are making *enchiladas* for several people, your best bet is to shallow-fry them, fill and roll up, then keep them warm. When they have all been made and you are ready to eat, bake them for 15 minutes covered with foil, and then add the boiling sauce and final garnish. If you are entertaining a large group, *Budin Azteca* (see page 121) would be a better choice, because it can be prepared ahead of time and, though different in appearance, is equally delicious.

In Mexico we use finely crumbled cheese. *Queso fresco* is very much like any of the English crumbly white cheeses but a little more salty. In the north of Mexico and in the USA, they like to melt the cheese. For this purpose, a mature Cheddar combined with some mozzarella gives the best results. In England, melted cheese is more popular and, although not as authentic, it is still quite delicious.

INGREDIENTS

oil

12 corn *tortillas* (see page 24)

1 onion, finely chopped

225 g (8 oz) *queso fresco* or white Cheshire cheese, crumbled

1 quantity *Salsa para Enchiladas* (see page 35)

1 lettuce, finely shredded, to garnish

METHOD

■ Heat the oil in a frying pan and flash-fry the *tortillas* for 3 seconds on each side, then drain on absorbent kitchen paper. Whilst still hot (this is important, because if the *tortilla* cools it will go tough), put about 1 teaspoon onion and 1 teaspoon crumbled cheese down the middle of the *tortilla* and roll it up. Keep in a warm place. Repeat this procedure until you have filled and rolled all the *tortillas*. Put the rolled *tortillas* in an ovenproof dish, cover with foil and bake in the oven at 180°C, 350°F, Gas Mark 4 for about 20 minutes. Spoon over the boiling hot sauce, sprinkle with the remaining onions and crumbled cheese, and serve immediately, garnished with shredded lettuce.

Enchiladas Anita

STUFFED *TORTILLAS* IN A CHILLI SAUCE

SERVES 8

These are a home favourite; my mother made them to perfection. It was always an occasion when my British grandmother came for lunch and we served these *enchiladas* at her request. They are meatless and very tasty; you can serve them as a main course or if you prefer as a side dish with roast pork.

INGREDIENTS

150 g (5 oz) *ancho* chillies	¹/₂ teaspoon salt
300 ml (¹/₂ pint) single cream	oil
¹/₂ onion, charred and coarsely chopped (see page 43)	8 corn *tortillas* (see page 24)
2 cloves garlic, charred	225 g (8 oz) *queso fresco* or Wensleydale cheese, crumbled
1 chicken stock cube	¹/₂ onion, very finely chopped
1 teaspoon sugar	

METHOD

■ Wash the *ancho* chillies in hot water to soften them a little. Remove the stalks and the seeds, then soak them in the cream for at least 2 hours. Put the chillies and cream in a blender with the coarsely chopped onion, the garlic and stock cube and blend to a paste. Strain and stir in the sugar and salt.

■ Heat some oil in a frying pan. Dip the *tortillas* in the cold sauce and flash-fry, one at a time, for 15 seconds on each side. As they are done, place them on a warm platter. Reserve a little cheese and finely chopped onion to garnish, and sprinkle the remainder over each fried *tortilla*. Fold each one in half and then in half again so it is fan-shaped. Arrange on a heated serving dish. When all the *enchiladas* have been fried, heat any sauce you have left in the pan, simmer for about 2 minutes and spoon over the folded *tortillas*. Sprinkle with the remaining cheese and onion before serving hot.

Enchiladas Suizas

—— *TORTILLAS* STUFFED WITH CHICKEN, CREAM AND CHEESE ——

SERVES 4

Swiss *Enchiladas* is yet another example of the international flavour of Mexico City and of the versatility of the *tortilla* which is equally delicious with its native sauces and garnishes as it is with foreign ingredients! *Enchiladas* are quick to prepare, provided the *tortillas* are already made. Green *Enchiladas Suizas* are served as a speciality at a well-known restaurant in Mexico City, which has made this dish famous. A birthday treat for me as a child was to be taken to Sanborn's for lunch. The *tortillas*, filled with cooked chicken and covered with generous quantities of sauce, cheese and cream, are baked in a hot oven and served with *Frijoles Refritos* and mixed salad. This could make a good informal dinner dish. For variety, I suggest using *Salsa Verde*, but a tomato sauce, or any of the dried chilli sauces, go equally well.

INGREDIENTS

8 tablespoons oil	100 g (4 oz) *queso de Chihuahua* or mature Cheddar cheese, grated
12 corn *tortillas* (see page 24)	100 g (4 oz) mozzarella cheese, grated
1/2 cooked chicken, boned, skinned and cut in large pieces	150 ml (1/4 pint) soured cream
1 quantity *Salsa de Tomate Verde* (see page 33) or any basic sauce	1/2 onion, finely chopped

METHOD

■ Heat the oil in a heavy-based frying pan and seal the *tortillas* by flash-frying for 3 seconds. Add more oil as required. Drain the *tortillas* on absorbent kitchen paper, stacking them up with layers of the paper. This helps to keep them warm as they drain off the extra oil. (If they go cold they become tough and will not roll.)

■ Fill each *tortilla* with cooked chicken pieces, roll up and place in an ovenproof dish. Ideally, you should use individual ovenproof dishes with three rolled *tortillas* per dish, but a 25 x 20 cm (10 x 8 inch) casserole will do. This can be done ahead of time. Cover tightly with foil and bake in a preheated oven at 190°C, 375°F, Gas Mark 5 for 20 minutes. Meanwhile, bring the sauce to the boil and mix the cheeses together. Uncover the *enchiladas*, pour boiling sauce over them, then the cream and sprinkle with cheese and onion. Return to the oven for a few minutes until the cheese melts. Serve immediately.

Taquitos de Cascara de Papa

—— CORN *TORTILLAS* FILLED WITH STEWED POTATO SKINS ——

SERVES 6

These *taquitos* were great favourites of my mother's and we used to enjoy them when we were alone, as eating potato skins in those days had almost a social stigma. Twenty-five years on, and we are eating potato skins because of their food value, texture and fibre. These *taquitos* are always made with soft, warm *tortillas* – corn are my favourite, but wheat are good too. (To reheat *tortillas*, see page 26). Make the *taquitos* a little hot as the 'bite' enhances the flavour.

INGREDIENTS

1 kg (2 lb) potatoes	¹/₂ teaspoon salt
2 tablespoons oil	¹/₂ teaspoon ground black pepper
6 spring onions, coarsely chopped	4 tablespoons water
6 tomatoes, charred, peeled and chopped (see page 43)	eighteen 15 cm (6 inch) corn or wheat flour *tortillas* (see pages 24–7)
3 green chillies, sliced	
4 sprigs fresh *epazote* or coriander, coarsely chopped	

METHOD

■ Scrub the potatoes, then peel them fairly thickly so that some of the potato is attached to the skin. Heat the oil in a frying pan and sauté the potato skins, spring onions, tomatoes, chillies, *epazote* or coriander, salt and pepper. Add the water, cover tightly and simmer for 10 minutes. Serve hot and let everyone make their own *taquitos* with hot *tortillas*. Put 1 tablespoon filling in the centre of a *tortilla*, roll up and eat by hand. Make the next *taquito* when you are ready to eat it.

Tacos de Rajas Poblanas

TACOS OR *FAJITAS* FILLED WITH PEPPERS AND ONIONS

SERVES 4

Rajas means chillies cut lengthways. This is a very popular filling for *tortillas*, a colourful side dish and easy to prepare.

INGREDIENTS

1 tablespoon oil	¹/₄ teaspoon ground black pepper
1 large onion, finely sliced	1 tablespoon chopped fresh *epazote* or coriander
2 *chiles poblanos* or green peppers, charred, peeled, deseeded and cut into strips (see page 42)	2 tablespoons tomato purée
2 green chillies, finely sliced (if using green peppers)	100 ml (4 fl oz) *Caldo* (see page 40) or 1 chicken stock cube diluted in 100 ml (4 fl oz) water
100 g (4 oz) corn kernels (optional)	¹/₄ teaspoon lemon juice
100 g (4 oz) mushrooms, sliced (optional)	corn or wheat flour *tortillas* (see pages 24–7), to serve
¹/₂ teaspoon salt	

METHOD

■ Heat the oil in a heavy-based frying pan and fry the onion, peppers, chillies, corn and mushrooms, if using, for about 3 minutes, stirring frequently. Add the remaining ingredients. Stir, then cover tightly and cook for 2 minutes over medium heat. Serve with hot corn or wheat flour *tortillas*.

Chalupas

BOAT-SHAPED CORN *TORTILLAS*

SERVES 4

Chalupas are named after the flat boats which were used in the canals of old Tenochtitlán, now Mexico City. In Xochimilco, the floating gardens in the south of the city, you can still see these beautiful flat boats which are filled with flowers, food and Mexican curios, the vendors sitting amongst their wares.

Chalupas are cooked in a similar way to *Tortillas de Maiz* (see page 24), but the edge of each *tortilla* is pinched into a ridge all the way round to hold the sauce while the *tortilla* is still hot off the griddle. *Chalupas* must be eaten hot, and make an excellent starter. The boats may be prepared in advance and the filling and garnish added just before serving.

INGREDIENTS

¼ **quantity corn tortilla dough (see page 24)**	**225 g (8 oz) white cheese, such as Wensleydale or white Cheshire, crumbled**
6 tablespoons oil	**1 small onion, finely chopped**
1 quantity *Salsa de Tomate Verde* (see page 33), *Salsa para Enchiladas* (see page 35) or *Salsa Adobada* (see page 36)	**1 small lettuce, very finely shredded**

METHOD

■ Form the *tortilla* dough into eight cigar shapes about 10 cm (4 inches) long, and 2.5 cm (1 inch) in diameter. Place on waxed (not greaseproof) paper squares, as for *tortillas* (see page 24) but positioned diagonally. Cover with waxed paper and press lightly to a thickness of 3 mm (¹/₈ inch). (If you do not have a *tortilla* press, roll lightly with a rolling pin between two squares of waxed paper, or press with the base of your hand.) Grill on both sides as for *tortillas*. While the *tortilla* is still hot, pinch the edge into a ridge all the way round, using thumb and forefinger. If this is not done immediately after cooking, it will be impossible to form the ridge. Keep the *Chalupas* warm in a tea-towel.

■ Heat the oil in a heavy-based frying pan and fry each *Chalupa*, ridge side up, basting with hot oil to seal the top. Fill each *Chalupa* with 2 tablespoons sauce, crumbled cheese and chopped onion, and serve immediately, garnished with shredded lettuce.

Enfrijoladas

TORTILLAS WITH BEANS, CHEESE AND SAUCE

SERVES 4

*E*nfrijoladas describes *tortillas* liberally spread with refried beans and topped with any type of *salsa* and cheese, cream, lettuce, crispy *chorizo*, or anything that you have at hand. Leftover meat, fried until crisp is also very good. *Enfrijoladas* make a good starter or light meal, but double the recipe for the latter.

INGREDIENTS

1 tablespoon oil	225 g (8 oz) *Frijoles Refritos* (see page 31)
¼ onion, chopped	8 tablespoons *salsa*
1 green chilli, finely chopped	50 g (2 oz) crumbly white cheese
150 g (5 oz) shredded cooked meat or crispy fried *chorizo*	2 spring onions, thinly sliced
	Jalapeños en Vinagre (see page 176)
4 corn *tortillas* (see page 24)	

METHOD

■ If using leftover meat, heat the oil in a frying pan and sauté the onion and chilli. Add the meat and fry, stirring frequently, until it turns dark brown and crispy. Remove from the pan and drain on absorbent kitchen paper. Spread each *tortilla* with a generous helping of *Frijoles Refritos*, and shallow-fry gently, spooning a little hot oil on the beans. The *tortilla* should become crispy on the bottom but remain moist on top because you do not turn it over. Top with crispy meat, *salsa*, cheese, onions and *Jalapeños*. Serve immediately.

Garnachas

MAIZE BITES WITH PORK AND *SALSA*

MAKES 12
5 cm (2 inch)
garnachas

Like *sopes*, *garnachas* are popular before meals. They are ideal for using up leftover pork with any of the *salsas* but *Salsa de Chile Chilpotle* (see page 38) goes particularly well.

INGREDIENTS

120 g (4¹/₂ oz) *masa harina* (see page 19)	200 g (7 oz) cooked pork, shredded and lightly fried
50 g (2 oz) plain flour	
1 tablespoon baking powder	100 g (4 oz) hot cooked potatoes, diced
¹/₂ teaspoon salt	250 ml (8 fl oz) hot *salsa* (see above)
1 tablespoon lard	oil
150 ml (¹/₄ pint) water	¹/₂ onion, finely chopped, to garnish

METHOD

■ Mix together the dry ingredients, rub in the lard and blend in the water. Knead for about 5 minutes to a soft dough, then divide up and press as for *tortillas* (see page 24). If you have not got a press, flatten a walnut-sized ball of dough between your moistened palms until it is about 5 cm (2 inches) in diameter and thick enough to handle easily. Cook on a hot griddle, turning only once. Repeat until all the dough is finished.

■ Before serving, shallow-fry each *garnacha* in hot oil for 1 minute. Drain and place on a serving plate. Spread some meat and potato over it and lace it with hot *salsa*. Garnish with chopped onion.

Sopes De Colima

—— CORN *TORTILLA* 'BOWLS' WITH BEANS AND *CHORIZO* ——

ᴧᴧᴧ

MAKES 32
5 cm (2 inch)
sopes (Serves 8)

Sopes are a very popular starter in Mexico and every region offers its own variation. These *sopes* have chillies added to the dough before shaping. In some of the hotels in Mexico City a girl dressed in regional costume shapes and cooks *Sopes* at the bar in front of the guests. The smell of them gently frying ensures that all her food will be consumed as it is impossible to resist ordering some. They are a typical example of an *antojito*.

INGREDIENTS

375 g (13 oz) *masa harina* (see page 19)	600 ml (1 pint) *salsa* (any type)
250 g (9 oz) plain flour	1 small lettuce, very finely chopped
1 tablespoon baking powder	100 g (4 oz) *chorizo*, fried and crumbled
1 egg	250 g (9 oz) *queso fresco* or white Cheshire cheese, crumbled
3 green chillies	
oil	2 avocados
300 ml (¹/₂ pint) warm water	10 radishes, finely sliced
400 g (14 oz) warm *Frijoles Refritos* (see page 31)	100 g (4 oz) soured cream or yoghurt

METHOD

■ Mix the flours and the baking powder together in the bowl of an electric mixer. Put the egg, chillies and 1 tablespoon oil in a blender and work to a smooth paste. Add to the flours and mix with the dough hook. Add the water and continue mixing to make a very solid dough that sticks to the hook and leaves the sides of the bowl clean.

■ Heat a heavy-based griddle or frying pan. Divide the dough into 16 even-sized balls and put them in a polythene bag or cover them with cling film. Flatten one ball of dough at a time between the palms of your moistened hands to a round about 5 cm (2 inches) in diameter and about 1 cm (¹/₂ inch) thick. Place on the very hot griddle and cook for 1¹/₂ minutes on each side. Remove from the heat and keep warm by wrapping in a clean tea-towel. Repeat until all the dough balls are cooked.

■ While the *sopes* are still hot, insert the point of a sharp knife in the side of each one and cut in half, much as you would cut a scone in half. The middle of the *sopes* will still be uncooked. With your thumb and forefinger, push the soft dough towards the edges to create a ridge all the way around.

■ Spread both halves of each *sope* with warm refried beans. Heat about 1 cm ($^1/_2$ inch) oil in a heavy-based frying pan and fry four or five *sopes*, beans uppermost, for about 45 seconds. They will become crunchy underneath and moist on top. Drain on absorbent kitchen paper and keep warm. When all the *sopes* are fried, top each one with *salsa*, lettuce, *chorizo*, crumbled cheese, avocado wedges and sliced radishes and soured cream or yoghurt. Eat immediately.

Pambacitos Compuestos

——— CRUSTY ROLLS IN A CHILLI SAUCE ———

᭝᭝᭝

SERVES 4

Pambacitos Compuestos are bread rolls filled with potato and *chorizo* in a chilli sauce. *Pambazo* is the name of the particular type of bread traditionally used, but if it is not available, small pitta breads are a good substitute. This snack is quick to put together, provided you have some *Salsa Adobada* ready made. In Mexico, it is often served for brunch but it makes a good supper or light lunch dish with a green salad and some beans.

INGREDIENTS

4 small pitta breads	pinch of salt and ground black pepper
3 tablespoons oil	$^1/_2$ quantity *Salsa Adobada* (see page 36)
100 g (4 oz) *chorizo*, chopped	$^1/_2$ small lettuce, finely shredded
2 large potatoes, boiled and cubed	

METHOD

■ Cut a slit in the side of each pitta bread. Heat 1 tablespoon oil in a frying pan and fry the *chorizo* for about 7 minutes or until crisp. Add the cooked potato, salt and pepper and heat through, stirring, for 4 minutes. Drain and keep warm.

■ Fill the breads with the potato mixture and some of the lettuce, reserving some for garnish. If necessary, secure with cocktail sticks. Heat the remaining oil in the frying pan. Dip one pitta bread into the cold *Salsa*, then fry on each side for about 3 minutes. Remove from the heat, discard the cocktail stick and keep warm while frying the other filled pitta breads. Heat any leftover *salsa* in the pan, spoon it over the breads and serve immediately, garnished with shredded lettuce.

Taco Shells

CRISP *TORTILLA* SHELLS

SERVES 6

*T*aco shells are an American invention, though something similar is made in the north of Mexico by just folding a *tortilla* in half after it has been filled. The American idea of deep-frying *tortillas* in this shape has not generally been adopted by Mexicans, and I doubt it ever will. Home-made *taco* shells are not as perfect in shape as bought ones but they are nicer and add character. They can be fried several days in advance, provided they are stored in an airtight container. They even freeze well.

Taco fillings can be anything you wish, but the most popular are shredded lettuce, cooked chicken, *guacamole* and soured cream, as in this recipe; or shredded lettuce with *picadillo*, soured cream, cheese and *jalapeños en vinagre*, or the inevitable *chilli con carne* with soured cream and cheese. They can be served as starters, or if you make miniatures, they can be offered with drinks. Always use fresh or frozen corn *tortillas* and feel free to substitute strained Greek yoghurt for the cream.

INGREDIENTS

oil for deep-frying	1 quantity *Guacamole* (see page 48)
12 corn *tortillas* (see page 24)	75 ml (3 fl oz) soured cream or strained Greek yoghurt
FILLING	*jalapeños en Vinagre* (see page 176)
1 small lettuce, very finely shredded	
3 cooked skinless chicken breasts, shredded	

METHOD

■ Heat the oil in a deep-fryer to 180°C, 350°F. Place one *tortilla* in the hot oil, holding it with tongs in a 'U' shape by pressing it against the side of the pan. Cook the *tortilla* in this position for about 1 minute, then let it go and fry for another 3 minutes until golden brown. The *tortilla* should keep its shape; if it doesn't, you are not holding it for long enough with the tongs. Drain the *tortilla*, upside down, on absorbent kitchen paper. Fry the remaining *tortillas* in the same way. These *taco* shells can be used at room temperature without reheating, but if they have been stored and have lost their freshness, reheat them in a moderate oven for 10 minutes to freshen them up.

■ To fill the warm shells, divide the lettuce generously between them. Add the chicken, then spoon some *Guacamole* over the top, followed by a little soured cream and *jalapeños en vinagre*. If you are using other fillings, always put the lettuce in first, then the meat and finally the toppings. Once filled, *taco* shells should be eaten within 30 minutes because the moisture from the filling softens them; although they will still be palatable, the filling might drop out!

VARIATION

To make miniature *taco* shells, use a biscuit cutter to cut the fresh *tortillas* into 7.5 cm (3 inch) circles, then fry in the same way. The trimmings can be fried for *Totopos* (see page 46).

Tostadas Compuestas

—— CRISPY FRIED CORN *TORTILLAS* WITH SALAD TOPPING ——

SERVES 6

*T*ostadas are one of Mexico's most picturesque dishes, and they are nutritious too! To add atmosphere to a party and help break the ice – that is, if the *tequila* cocktail hasn't done it for you – you can lay out all the ingredients and let your guests assemble their own *tostadas*.

The size of the *tostada* depends on the size of the *tortilla* you use. Small *tortillas*, 7.5 cm (3 inches) in diameter, are less forbidding than larger ones. This recipe calls for 15 cm (6 inches) *tortillas*, which make a good starter. With so many ingredients and textures, you will not miss the meat if you prefer to make this a vegetarian dish by omitting the chicken. The *tostadas* can be fried up to a week in advance but must be kept in an airtight container once cooled.

INGREDIENTS

six 15 cm (6 inch) corn *tortillas* (see page 24)

oil for deep-frying

225 g (8 oz) *Frijoles Refritos* (see page 31), cooled

1 small crisp lettuce, finely shredded

225 g (8 oz) cooked chicken, boned and shredded

12 slices of tomato

12 onion rings

6 tablespoons soured cream

2 tablespoons milk

50 g (2 oz) *queso fresco* or white Cheshire cheese, crumbled

1 quantity *Guacamole* (see page 48) or 1 avocado

jalapeños en vinagre (see page 176)

salt and ground black pepper

METHOD

■ Deep-fry the *tortillas* in very hot oil for 2–3 minutes or until golden brown. *Tostadas* need not be entirely flat, so don't worry if the *tortillas* curl slightly as you fry them; use a slotted spoon and a fork to flatten them. If they start to puff up, just flatten the bubble with the back of the spoon. Drain on absorbent kitchen paper.

■ When all the *tortillas* are fried, spread each one with beans and top with lettuce, chicken, tomato slices, onion rings, soured cream thinned with milk, crumbled cheese, *Guacamole* or avocado slices and *jalapeños en vinagre*. Season lightly with salt and pepper. Eat within 20 minutes; they are best eaten by hand with a large plate beneath!

Indios Vestidos

TORTILLAS IN BATTER AND TOMATO OR CHILLI SAUCE

SERVES 4

The literal translation of *Indios Vestidos* is 'dressed Indians', the 'dress' being a coating of egg! In any case, it is a very good alternative to traditional *Peneques* which are extremely difficult to make and impossible to obtain outside Mexico. This dish makes a good starter or light lunch accompanied by *frijoles refritos*. If you cannot find *ancho* chillies, try this dish with *Salsa para Enchiladas* (see page 35) instead, omitting the first four and the last four ingredients.

INGREDIENTS

2 *ancho* chillies	3 tablespoons oil
450 ml (³/₄ pint) boiling chicken stock	2 tablespoons flour
1 clove garlic	1 onion, finely chopped
¹/₄ teaspoon ground cinnamon	2 tablespoons tomato purée
6 corn *tortillas* (see page 24)	¹/₂ teaspoon salt
175 g (6 oz) Cheddar cheese, coarsely grated	¹/₄ teaspoon sugar
2 eggs, separated	

METHOD

■ Heat the *ancho* chillies in a dry heavy-based frying pan for about 2 minutes on each side or until they soften. Remove and discard the stems, seeds and veins, and place the chillies in a bowl. Cover with boiling stock and leave to soak for 30 minutes.

■ Put the garlic, chillies, stock and cinnamon in a blender and work to a thick paste. Set aside.

■ Cut the *tortillas* in half and warm them through in a heavy-based frying pan for about 30 seconds on each side. Place some grated cheese (reserving a little for garnish) on each *tortilla* half, then fold over to form a triangle, securing with a cocktail stick. Beat the egg yolks until pale and fluffy. In a separate bowl, whisk the whites until stiff, then blend in the yolks.

■ Heat the oil in a frying pan. Dip each filled *tortilla* in flour, then in the egg, and fry until light golden. Drain on absorbent kitchen paper. Fry the onion in the pan until soft, then add the tomato purée, salt and sugar. Sieve the chilli mixture into the pan and simmer for about 15 minutes.

■ Remove the cocktail sticks from the *tortillas* and place the *tortillas* in an ovenproof dish. Cover and bake in the oven at 180°C, 350°F, Gas Mark 4 for 20 minutes. Bring the sauce to the boil and pour it over the *tortillas* before serving garnished with the reserved cheese.

Moyetes

―――― CRUSTY ROLLS WITH REFRIED BEANS AND CHEESE ――――

SERVES 4

Moyetes can be served on their own or alongside any egg dish for breakfast. They are the Mexican version of open sandwiches – a quick snack, provided the beans are already refried.

INGREDIENTS

4 crusty bread rolls, halved	¹/₂ quantity *Salsa de Jitomate Típica* (see page 34)
25 g (1 oz) butter	1 avocado
275 g (10 oz) *Frijoles Refritos* (see page 31)	salt and ground black pepper
50 g (2 oz) Cheddar cheese, grated	

METHOD

■ Remove the dough from the centres of the crusty rolls, butter them and spread liberally with refried beans. Cover with grated cheese and bake in the oven at 170°C, 325°F, Gas Mark 3 for 20 minutes. Spoon some sauce over each roll half and arrange a slice of avocado on top. Season with salt and pepper, and serve immediately.

Tortas Compuestas

―――――――― FILLED CRUSTY ROLLS ――――――――

SERVES 4

Mexican 'sandwiches', *Tortas Compuestas*, are made with miniature French loaves called *bolillos* or *teleras* and filled with anything available – sliced cooked meats, such as ham, steak, roast beef, pork or chicken; scrambled eggs; cheese, etc. and a combination of refried beans, avocado slices, soured cream, sliced tomatoes, lettuce and hot chilli pickles. Usually one is enough to satisfy you but you are more likely to eat two because they are so delicious!

INGREDIENTS

4 medium-sized crusty bread rolls or 1 French stick, cut into 4	2 tomatoes, sliced
¹/₂ quantity warm *Frijoles Refritos* (see page 31)	¹/₂ onion, finely sliced
	2 avocados
1 lettuce, finely shredded	salt and ground black pepper
4 slices of Cheddar cheese	*jalapeños en Vinagre* (see page 176)
4 slices of cooked meat or chicken	100 ml (4 fl oz) soured cream

METHOD   ■ Warm the bread in the oven at 180°C, 350°F, Gas Mark 4 for about 15 minutes to make it nice and crusty. Cut each roll or portion of French bread in half and discard the soft doughy centre if necessary. Cover the bottom half with warm beans, lettuce, cheese and meat. Arrange tomato, onion and avocado slices on top, and season with salt and pepper. Top with *jalapeños*. Spread the top half of each roll with soured cream, place, cream-side down, on top of the chillies, and eat immediately.

Pepitos

BEEF AND AVOCADO SANDWICHES

SERVES 4   *Pepitos*, not to be confused with *pepitas* (pumpkin seeds), are a type of *torta*. Like *tacos*, *tortas* are snacks often eaten on the street. Literally translated, *pepito* means 'little Joe' which is not at all surprising because in Mexico all men are christened Joseph before any chosen name and all women are christened Mary before their chosen name. So this is a steak and avocado sandwich with a proper first name!

INGREDIENTS

4 crusty bread rolls or 1 French stick, cut into 4	2 ripe avocados
French mustard	salt and ground black pepper
225 g (8 oz) *Frijoles Refritos* (see page 31)	*Jalapeños en Vinagre* (see page 176)
4 slices of cold roast beef	

METHOD   ■ Warm the bread in the oven at 180°C, 350°F, Gas Mark 4 for 15 minutes. Cut each roll or piece of French bread in half and discard the soft doughy centres. Spread mustard and beans on the bottom half of each roll, and top with beef. Stone, peel and mash the avocados and spread over the beef. Season with salt and pepper, and top with *jalapeños*. Cover with the remaining bread halves and eat immediately.

Panuchos Yucatecos

CORN *TORTILLAS* FILLED WITH BEANS AND TOPPED WITH CHICKEN

SERVES 4

*P*anuchos is almost a Yucatecan word as it does not describe any other dish in the culinary repertoire of the country. They are a sort of *tostada* and make good snacks or starters. They are very popular along the coast as far off as Veracruz, and are the sort of *antojitos* that are prepared and shallow-fried in the streets and plazas. This dish can only be made with home-made *tortillas*, pressed a little thicker than usual and cooked in the traditional way, turning them for a third time until they puff.

INGREDIENTS

twelve 10 cm (4 inch) home-made *tortillas* (see pages 24–7)	2 cooked skinless chicken breasts, shredded
¹/₂ quantity warm refried black beans (Frijoles Refritos, see page 31)	*jalapeños en Vinagre* (see page 176)
3 hard-boiled eggs, sliced	shredded lettuce, to garnish
6 tablespoons oil	

METHOD

■ Carefully lift the thin layer on top of each *tortilla*, thus creating a pocket. With a spatula, spread the insides of the pockets with warm beans and place slices of boiled egg over the beans.

■ When all the *tortillas* are filled, heat the oil in a frying pan and fry the *tortillas*, thicker side down, for about 3 minutes or until they start to turn golden. Remove them from the pan and drain on absorbent kitchen paper. Cover the top of each *tortilla* with shredded chicken and a little *jalapeños en vinagre*. Garnish with lettuce and serve immediately.

OPPOSITE   Clockwise from top: *Chocolate Caliente* (drinking chocolate, page 195), *Huevos Revueltos con Chorizo* (scrambled eggs with spicy sausage, page 103) and *Pan de Muerto* (Hallowe'en bread, page 188)

Papadzules

YUCATECAN *ENCHILADAS* FILLED WITH EGG AND PUMPKIN SEEDS

ᴧᴧᴧ

SERVES 8

*P*apadzules is a Mayan name given to a dish composed of corn *tortillas* filled with hard-boiled eggs and topped with *chiltomate* (tomato sauce). In simple terms, it is an egg *enchilada* – an original vegetarian dish. Pumpkin seeds are available from large supermarkets, health food shops or Chinese super-markets, but if you cannot get them try using shelled almonds instead. If anything, the results are even more delicious.

INGREDIENTS

275 g (10 oz) pumpkin seeds, shelled, or chopped almonds	3 cloves garlic, charred and crushed (see page 43)
3 green chillies	salt
2 sprigs fresh *epazote* or coriander	twenty-four 7.5 cm (3 inch) corn *tortillas* (see page 24)
600 ml (1 pint) warm water	
1 onion, charred and quartered (see page 43)	8 eggs, hard-boiled and sliced
	$^1/_2$ quantity *Salsa para Enchiladas* (see page 35)

METHOD

■ Roast the pumpkin seeds in a dry frying pan for 5 minutes, stirring constantly. Place them in a blender or food processor with the chillies and *epazote* or coriander, and grind to a powder. Transfer to a bowl. Put the water in a saucepan, add the onion and garlic, and bring to the boil. Season with salt and boil for about 15 minutes. Strain and discard the vegetables.

■ Add the water to the powdered pumpkin seeds, a little at a time, then pour the mixture into a saucepan. Heat gently without boiling, stirring constantly, until the sauce is thick enough to coat the back of the spoon. (If the sauce boils and curdles, return it to the food processor and reheat in a double saucepan.)

■ Flash-fry the *tortillas* and dip into the hot pumpkin sauce. Top with the hard-boiled egg, roll up and arrange in a serving dish. In a separate saucepan, warm up the *Salsa*. Pour the remaining pumpkin seed sauce over the top of the *Papadzules* and cover with the *Salsa*.

OPPOSITE   Left to right: *Pico de Gallo* (fruit and vegetable salad, page 174) and *Mole Poblano* (turkey in rich chilli and chocolate sauce, page 122) served with *Arroz Blanco* (white rice, page 98)

SOUPS

▲▲▲▲▲▲▲▲▲▲▲▲▲▲▲▲▲

MEXICANS enjoy two types of soup. The first, *sopa aguada* (liquid soup),
is a dish that dates from colonial days. It is served hot throughout the year,
and despite the heat in the middle of the day, no Mexican meal is complete
without it. A good *caldo* (stock) is of utmost importance, and beans,
avocados, pumpkin blossoms, *tortilla* chips and fresh and dried chillies
provide a diversity of flavours and textures.

The second type of 'soup' is less common. Called *sopa seca* (dry soup), it
consists of rice or pasta and is sometimes served as a separate course after
the *sopa aguada*. Pasta soups like *Sopa Seca de Fideo or Sopa de Macarrón con
Queso* are of Italian origin, while *arroz* (rice) was introduced into the
Mexican diet by the Spaniards. Rice is more commonly served as an
accompaniment or side dish, to be eaten as part of the main course, so this
chapter does not include any rice 'soups'. See the following chapter for
other types of rice dishes.

Caldo Tlalpeño

CHICKEN SOUP WITH AVOCADO

SERVES 6

This is such a popular soup that it is found up and down the country. For a light lunch it goes very well accompanied by *Quesadillas* (see pages 58–63).

INGREDIENTS

6 corn *tortillas* (see page 24)	2 green chillies, chopped
oil	¼ teaspoon black pepper
1.7 litres (3 pints) *Caldo* (see page 40)	2 tablespoons chopped fresh coriander
2 skinless chicken breast fillets, boiled and shredded	1 lime, cut into 8 wedges
3 avocados	

METHOD

■ Unless the *tortillas* are already stale, cut them into strips and leave them uncovered overnight. Break them into bite-sized pieces. Heat some oil in a frying pan, and fry the *tortilla* pieces until golden. Drain on absorbent kitchen paper.

■ Put the *Caldo* in a saucepan and bring to the boil. Add the cooked chicken and simmer for 5 minutes. Stone, peel and slice the avocados. Place the *tortilla* pieces in six individual bowls and pour over the boiling *Caldo* and chicken meat. Serve garnished with avocado slices, chillies, black pepper and coriander, with wedges of lime on the side. (The sharpness of the lime enhances the flavour of the soup.)

Sopa Aguada de Fideo

VERMICELLI SOUP

SERVES 4

This is another hot soup with a *Caldo* base. I find this a good soup to make when I have leftover *vermicelli*. It is a light, hot starter.

INGREDIENTS

1 quantity *Caldo* (see page 40) or 2 chicken stock cubes dissolved in 1 litre (1³/₄ pints) boiling water

3 tablespoons tomato purée

1 onion, finely chopped

100 g (4 oz) cooked *vermicelli* or 50 g (2 oz) dried *vermicelli* or other fine pasta

1 tablespoon finely chopped fresh parsley

¹/₄ teaspoon ground black pepper

¹/₂ lemon, quartered

METHOD

■ Place all the ingredients except the lemon, in a saucepan. Bring to the boil then reduce the heat and simmer for 20 minutes. Serve hot with the lemon wedges, adding a few drops of juice at the last minute.

Sopa De Frijol Negro

BLACK BEAN SOUP

SERVES 6

Bean soup is a favourite in all its varied preparations. The flavour changes slightly with the type of bean used, but it is a hearty, thick soup, excellent for winter meals. *Epazote* (*Chenopodium ambrosioides*) grows easily in England – outside in the summer and inside in the winter. If you plant it in a sheltered position in your garden, it will even come back year after year. The seeds can be bought from speciality seeds suppliers. *Epazote* also dries and keeps it flavour extremely well. It is a must with black beans. You can use fresh coriander if *epazote* is not available; and use milk instead of *Caldo* for a vegetarian soup.

INGREDIENTS

450 ml (³/₄ pint) black *Frijoles* (see page 28)	4 tablespoons chopped fresh *epazote* or coriander, or 2 tablespoons dried *epazote*, crumbled
¹/₂ onion, quartered	
600 ml (1 pint) *Caldo* (see page 40) or milk	¹/₄ teaspoon salt
4 tablespoons oil	¹/₄ teaspoon ground black pepper
1 clove garlic	pinch of sugar
1¹/₂ tablespoons tomato purée	1¹/₂ slices stale bread cut into 1 cm (¹/₂ inch) cubes
1 green chilli, chopped	

METHOD

■ Put the beans and onion in a blender or food processor with half the *Caldo* or milk, and work to a smooth paste. Heat 1 tablespoon oil in a saucepan and fry the garlic until black. Discard the garlic and sieve the bean mixture carefully into the pan. Add the remaining *Caldo* or milk and the tomato purée, chilli, *epazote* or coriander, salt, pepper and sugar. Simmer, uncovered, stirring frequently, for 20 minutes or until it thickens.

■ To make the croûtons, put the bread cubes on a baking tray and bake in the oven at 180°C, 350°F, Gas Mark 4 for 15 minutes or until golden. Alternatively, use the remaining 3 tablespoons oil and fry the bread, stirring constantly, until golden. Drain on absorbent kitchen paper and keep warm. Serve the soup in individual bowls and garnish with the croûtons.

Sopa De Flor De Calabaza

COURGETTE BLOSSOM SOUP

SERVES 4

If you have had the patience to save the blossoms from your courgette or marrow plants, and have a reasonable amount in the freezer, you can now surprise everyone with this lovely soup. *Queso pera* can be obtained from any Italian delicatessen and is a good substitute for *Queso de Oaxaca.*

INGREDIENTS

900 ml (1¹/₂ pints) *Caldo* (see page 40)	1 tablespoon chopped fresh *epazote* or coriander
100 g (4 oz) corn kernels, fresh or frozen	50 g (2 oz) mushrooms, sliced
15 g ('/₂ oz) butter	225 g (8 oz) courgette blossoms or 100 g (4 oz) raw spinach, chopped
¹/₂ onion, finely chopped	
1 clove garlic, crushed	2 tablespoons *queso de Oaxaca* or *queso pera*, shredded
1 tablespoon tomato purée	

METHOD

■ Put the *Caldo* in a saucepan and bring to the boil. Add the corn and boil for 5 minutes. Heat the butter in a frying pan and sauté the onion and garlic until soft. Add the tomato purée, *epazote* or coriander, mushrooms and blossoms or spinach and sauté for a further 5 minutes. Add this mixture to the *Caldo* and serve hot, garnished with shredded cheese.

Menudo

TRIPE AND CHILLI SOUP

᰷

SERVES 8

Menudo is enjoyed in most of Mexico in much the same way as *soupe à l'oignon* is enjoyed in France, except this soup is a complete meal in one. Tripe is very popular in Mexico where it is also eaten as a main course. It is considered a good remedy for hangovers, so this is just the soup to prepare ahead of time for New Year's Day when you might not feel like cooking. Tripe prepared in this manner is quite delicious and no different to, say, tongue, so don't let the thought of it put you off. It should be served in large bowls.

INGREDIENTS

450 g (1 lb) tripe, cut into small pieces	2 leeks, sliced
3.4 litres (6 pints) water	$^1/_2$ teaspoon ground black pepper
1 pig's trotter	$^1/_2$ teaspoon salt
2 bay leaves	TO SERVE
6 peppercorns	4 *jalapeño* chillies, sliced
4 sticks celery, roughly chopped	6 spring onions, chopped
5 cloves garlic	4 tablespoons finely chopped fresh coriander
2 carrots, roughly chopped	
225 g (8 oz) potatoes, peeled and diced	2 lemons, quartered
400 g (14 oz) *Maiz Cacahuazintle* (see page 32), canned hominy, drained, or frozen corn kernels	2 avocados
	Tortillas (see pages 24–7)
450 g (1 lb) canned peeled tomatoes, mashed	Guacamole (see page 48)

METHOD

■ Wash the tripe carefully and place it in a saucepan with the water, pig's trotter, bay leaves, peppercorns, celery, garlic and carrots. Cover and simmer for about 4 hours or until the tripe is very tender. Skim off and discard the foam on the surface as necessary.

■ Remove the pig's trotter from the pan and pick off the meat. Discard the bay leaves, carrots and celery, remove the tripe and strain the broth. Boil the broth until reduced by half, then add the remaining ingredients. Cover and simmer for about 20 minutes or until the potatoes are tender. Return the trotter meat and tripe to the pan and simmer for a further 5 minutes. Serve boiling hot with small bowls of chillies, spring onions, chopped coriander, lemon quarters and avocado wedges, and accompanied by warm *tortillas* and *guacamole*.

Pozole Jalisciense

PORK AND HOMINY SOUP

SERVES 8

This is a very hearty soup, similar to a *pot-au-feu*. It can be prepared ahead of time and keeps well in the fridge or freezer. Serve it for a special occasion in large bowls. It has lots of garnishes which are easy to prepare and help to make a colourful display, so don't be put off by the amount of ingredients. *Pozole* is traditionally made with a pig's head, but I prefer to use hand of pork. *Maiz Cacahuazintle* hominy (see page 32), used in Mexico for this soup, is unobtainable ready-made in England so this recipe uses canned hominy or frozen sweetcorn. If, however, you are able to get the right maize, cook it as directed on page 32. It pops when cooked and floats in the soup like miniature white flowers.

INGREDIENTS

1 kg (2 lb) hand of pork, boned (bones reserved)

1 kg (2 lb) pork neck bones

1 pig's trotter

2 onions, sliced

4 cloves garlic

6 cabbage leaves, roughly chopped

2 carrots, roughly chopped

6 sticks celery, roughly chopped

2 tablespoons malt vinegar

1/2 teaspoon salt

1/2 teaspoon black pepper

2 bay leaves

3.4 litres (6 pints) cold water

100 g (4 oz) tomato purée

1 teaspoon dried oregano

400 g (14 oz) can of hominy, drained, or frozen sweetcorn kernels

GARNISHES

1/4 quantity *Salsa Adobada* (see page 36)

2 ripe avocados, stoned, peeled, sliced and sprinkled with lemon juice

6 green chillies, finely sliced

1 small lettuce, very finely shredded

1 bunch radishes, sliced

6 spring onions, finely chopped

16 sprigs fresh coriander, finely chopped

16 *tortillas*, crispy fried into *Totopos* (see page 46), or warm fresh corn *tortillas*

50 g (2 oz) cayenne pepper

2 limes or lemons, each cut into 8 pieces

METHOD

■ Wash the meat and all the bones, and place all the ingredients, except the oregano and hominy or sweetcorn, in a large saucepan. Bring quickly to the boil and skim off any froth that appears on the surface. Reduce the heat and simmer, partly covered, for about 2 hours or until the meat is tender.

■ Remove the meat from the pan and cut it into bite-sized pieces. Strain the broth and discard all the bones and vegetables. Put the broth in a bowl, cool and refrigerate overnight.

■ Next day, remove the congealed fat from the surface of the broth. Return the broth to the saucepan and add the meat, oregano and hominy or sweetcorn. Bring the soup to the boil and serve very hot in a soup tureen surrounded by all the garnishes in individual bowls. Guests can then help themselves to garnishes, sprinkling a little of each over their soup with a squeeze of lime or lemon juice.

Sopa Tarasca

BEAN AND *TORTILLA* SOUP

SERVES 6

Almost a complete meal in itself, this is a colourful and substantial soup with good texture and a variety of flavours. Any type of beans can be used.

INGREDIENTS

600 ml (1 pint) *Frijoles* (see page 28)	6 corn *tortillas* (see page 24), cut into strips
4 tomatoes, charred and peeled (see page 43)	3 *pasilla* or green chillies
½ onion, charred (see page 43)	¼ teaspoon ground black pepper
1 clove garlic, charred (see page 43)	pinch of salt
2.3 litres (4 pints) *Caldo* (see page 40)	100 g (4 oz) white Cheshire cheese, crumbled
2 tablespoons oil	

METHOD

■ Put the beans, tomatoes, onion and garlic in a blender with half the *Caldo*, and blend until smooth. Heat the oil in a frying pan and fry the *tortilla* strips until crispy. Drain on absorbent kitchen paper. In the same oil, fry the whole *pasilla* chillies until crisp. Remove from the heat, discard the seeds and stems, crumble the chillies and keep warm. (If green chillies are used instead of *pasilla*, deseed and slice before frying.)

■ Sieve the bean mixture into the saucepan, add the remaining *Caldo*, pepper and salt, and simmer for 15 minutes or until the soup thickens. Serve the soup in warm bowls and garnish with *tortilla* strips, chillies and cheese.

Sopa de Elote con Rajas Poblanas

SWEETCORN AND CAPSICUM SOUP

SERVES 4

This is a creamy, tasty soup, good for a light lunch or as a starter for a formal meal. The *chiles poblanos* give it its traditional slightly hot flavour; if you cannot find *poblanos*, add a little sliced green chilli to the green pepper strips.

INGREDIENTS

600 ml (1 pint) milk	2 chicken stock cubes
300 ml ('/2 pint) water	15 g ('/2 oz) butter or margarine
225 g (8 oz) corn kernels	'/4 onion, finely chopped
1 *chile poblano*, charred (see page 42), peeled, deseeded and sliced	1 tablespoon cornflour
1 green pepper, charred (see page 42), peeled, deseeded and sliced	

METHOD

■ Put the milk, water, corn, chilli, pepper and chicken stock cubes in a saucepan and simmer for 8 minutes. Strain, reserving the liquid and vegetables. Heat the butter in a separate saucepan and sauté the onions until soft. Stir in the cornflour, then gradually add the reserved liquid, stirring occasionally. Add the vegetables and bring the mixture to the boil. Serve hot.

Sopa de Poro y Papa

LEEK AND POTATO SOUP

SERVES 4

Quick and easy, yet full of goodness, this soup is a great favourite in my family.

INGREDIENTS

'/2 onion, finely chopped	2 tablespoons chopped fresh parsley
900 ml (1'/2 pints) *Caldo* (see page 40)	1 tablespoon tomato purée
2 potatoes, peeled and diced	'/4 teaspoon ground black pepper
2 leeks, sliced	

METHOD

■ Place all the ingredients in a saucepan, cover and simmer for 15 minutes or until the potato is cooked. Serve hot.

VARIATION

Crema de Poro y Papa (Cream of Leek and Potato Soup) Leave the soup to cool, then blend until smooth. Add 150 ml ($^1/_4$ pint) single cream. Garnish with chopped fresh parsley and serve at room temperature.

Sopa de Aguacate con Cerveza
BEER AND AVOCADO SOUP

SERVES 4

Served cold, this is a quick and original soup. Its flavour is slightly hot. It must be prepared 2–3 hours before required, covered in cling film and refrigerated. The more adventurous might like to add a dash of Tabasco sauce.

INGREDIENTS

2 ripe avocados, stoned, peeled and sliced	1 green chilli, roughly chopped
300 ml ($^1/_2$ pint) milk	1 teaspoon salt
225 ml (8 fl oz) Mexican beer or light lager	$^1/_4$ teaspoon black pepper
225 ml (8 fl oz) plain yoghurt	2 tomatoes, finely chopped, to garnish
3 spring onions, chopped	cayenne pepper for dusting
8 sprigs fresh coriander	

METHOD

■ Place all the ingredients, except the tomatoes and cayenne pepper, in a blender or food processor, and blend until smooth. Transfer the soup to a bowl, cover with cling film and refrigerate for 2–3 hours.

■ To serve, transfer the soup to individual bowls. Garnish with chopped tomato and dust lightly with cayenne pepper.

Sopa de Albondiguitas y Verduras

—————— MINIATURE MEATBALL AND VEGETABLE SOUP ——————

SERVES 6

Serve this unusual soup with warm corn or flour *tortillas* instead of bread.

INGREDIENTS

175 g (6 oz) minced beef	2 tablespoons oil
1 teaspoon malt vinegar	1 clove garlic
1/4 teaspoon salt	1/4 onion, finely chopped
1/4 teaspoon black pepper	1 quantity hot *Caldo* (see page 40) or 1 litre (1 3/4 pints) boiling water and 2 beef stock cubes
1 egg, beaten	
1 tablespoon chopped fresh parsley	
2 tablespoons breadcrumbs	2 tablespoons tomato purée

METHOD

■ Season the meat with the vinegar, salt and pepper. Mix in half the egg and half the parsley. Using floured hands, roll the meat mixture into small meatballs the size of hazelnuts. Dip the meatballs in the remaining egg, then toss them in the breadcrumbs.

■ Heat the oil in a frying pan and fry the garlic clove until it turns black. Remove the garlic from the pan, add the meatballs to the flavoured oil and fry until golden, turning them as required. Remove from the pan with a slotted spoon and drain on absorbent kitchen paper. Put 1/2 tablespoon of the oil from the frying pan in a saucepan and heat. Add the onion and sauté until soft, then add the hot *Caldo* (or boiling water and stock cubes) and tomato purée. Finally, add the meatballs to the stock, simmer for 5 minutes and serve hot sprinkled with the remaining parsley.

Caldo Gallego

BUTTER BEAN, HAM AND SPINACH SOUP

SERVES 4

Caldo Gallego is a hearty winter soup of Spanish origin. It is very popular and delicious.

INGREDIENTS

225 g (8 oz) dried butter beans	1 bay leaf
2.6 litres (4¹/₂ pints) water	225 g (8 oz) spinach, chopped
1 knuckle of ham	3 tablespoons tomato purée
1 clove garlic	1 medium onion, chopped
1 teaspoon salt	100 g (4 oz) *chorizo*
1 teaspoon sugar	

METHOD

■ Pick over and rinse the beans. Place in a large saucepan, add the water and leave to soak overnight. Next day, if there is less than 7.5 cm (3 inches) water above the beans, add more water. Add the ham knuckle, the garlic clove, salt, sugar and bay leaf, and simmer for about 1¹/₂ hours or until the beans are very soft and the meat is falling off the bone. Discard the garlic and the bay leaf. Remove the knuckle and discard the skin, fat and bones. Chop the ham and return to the pan. Add the spinach, tomato purée and onion and boil for a further 10 minutes. Meanwhile, fry the *chorizo* until crisp. Serve the soup in individual bowls, garnished with crumbled *chorizo*.

Sopa de Tortilla

TORTILLA SOUP

SERVES 4

When *tortillas* are stale, they can be used to make this soup and you can impress your guests with a brand new taste experience. If you are using fresh *tortillas*, preparation starts the night before. As it is now possible to buy ready-salted tortilla chips in supermarkets, you can use them and save yourself the trouble of frying the *tortillas*.

INGREDIENTS

4 corn *tortillas* (see page 24) or 50 g (2 oz) ready-salted *tortilla* chips	1 clove garlic
2 tablespoons oil	¹/₂ onion, finely chopped
900 ml (1¹/₂ pints) *Caldo* (see page 40)	700 g (1¹/₂ lb) tomato purée
1 *pasilla* chilli or 1 fresh chilli, sliced	1 avocado and finely chopped fresh coriander, to garnish

METHOD

■ If using fresh *tortillas*, cut them into 1 cm (¹/₂ inch) strips and leave uncovered overnight. If the *tortillas* are already dry, break them into bite-sized pieces. Heat the oil in a saucepan and fry the *tortilla* pieces until golden, then remove with a slotted spoon and drain on absorbent kitchen paper.

■ Bring 150 ml (¹/₄ pint) *Caldo* to the boil and pour over the *pasilla* chilli. Leave to soak for 30 minutes, then drain, reserving the *Caldo*. Remove and discard the stem and seeds from the chilli, and chop the chilli finely.

■ Add the garlic clove to the oil remaining in the saucepan, and fry until black, then remove and discard. Fry the onion for 3 minutes, then add the tomato purée and *Caldo*, and simmer for 15 minutes, skimming off any foam that comes to the surface.

■ Just before serving, place the fried *tortilla* pieces or ready-salted tortilla chips in four warm bowls. Bring the soup back to the boil and pour it into the bowls. Garnish with chopped chilli, avocado slices and chopped coriander.

Sopa Seca De Fideo

VERMICELLI SOUP

SERVES 4

*S*opa de Fideo is a *sopa seca* or 'dry' soup. *Vermicelli* can be purchased in most supermarkets; it is similar to spaghetti but much finer, and is usually sold rolled in small bundles or 'nests'. This recipe is an unusual way to use pasta, but the soup is tasty and quick to prepare. My family love it.

INGREDIENTS

6 tablespoons oil	4 sprigs fresh parsley
1 clove garlic	2 green chillies
100 g (4 oz) dried *vermicelli*	¼ teaspoon black pepper
½ onion, finely chopped	½ teaspoon salt
4 tablespoons tomato purée	1 tablespoon freshly grated Parmesan cheese
1 litre (1¾ pints) chicken stock	

METHOD

■ Heat the oil in a large frying pan and fry the garlic clove until black. Remove and discard the garlic. Add the *vermicelli* to the pan, and fry over low heat until golden brown, taking care not to let it burn. Drain the *vermicelli* on absorbent kitchen paper.

■ Drain all but 1 tablespoon oil from the pan and sauté the onion for 3 minutes. Add the tomato purée, chicken stock, parsley, chillies, pepper and salt, and simmer for about 3 minutes. Add the *vermicelli*, cover and simmer over low heat for 15–20 minutes, stirring occasionally, until the *vermicelli* is very soft, has doubled in size and all the liquid is absorbed.

■ Remove the parsley and chillies from the soup. Discard the parsley and chop the chillies. Pour the soup into warmed soup bowls. Garnish with chillies, sprinkle with cheese and serve hot. This dish keeps well refrigerated.

Sopa de Macarrón con Queso

SPAGHETTI IN TOMATO SAUCE WITH CHEESE

SERVES 4

Introduced by the Italians who settled in the highlands of Veracruz, Italian food is very popular throughout Mexico. Hence *macarrón* (spaghetti), *ravioles* (ravioli) come under the 'dry soup' category at the Mexican table. They are used as starters or as snacks, and can be prepared ahead of time, ready for baking just before serving.

INGREDIENTS

1 litre (1³/₄ pints) water	4 tablespoons tomato purée
1¹/₂ onions	¹/₄ teaspoon ground black pepper
1 bay leaf	¹/₂ teaspoon chopped fresh oregano
¹/₂ teaspoon salt	1 canned pimiento, sliced, or 1 red pepper, deseeded and sliced
pared rind of 1 lemon	
225 g (8 oz) dried spaghetti or other pasta	150 ml (¹/₄ pint) soured cream
75 g (3 oz) butter	175 g (6 oz) mature Cheddar cheese, grated
100 g (4 oz) button mushrooms, sliced	

METHOD

■ Put the water in a large saucepan. Add ¹/₂ onion, the bay leaf, salt and lemon rind, and bring to the boil. Add the pasta and cook for about 12 minutes or until it is just tender. Strain, reserving the liquid, and rinse the pasta under cold running water to prevent it sticking. Drain. Discard the onion, bay leaf and lemon rind.

■ Chop the remaining onion. Melt the butter in a frying pan and sauté the mushrooms and chopped onion for about 5 minutes. Add the tomato purée, black pepper and oregano. Stir in 400 ml (14 fl oz) of the reserved liquid. Simmer for 5 minutes, then add the pasta and remove from the heat.

■ Grease a shallow, 20 x 15 cm (8 x 6 inch) ovenproof dish and fill it with layers of the pasta mixture, pimiento, soured cream and cheese, finishing with cheese. Bake in the oven at 180°C, 350°F, Gas Mark 4 for 20 minutes.

RICE AND EGGS

▲▲▲▲▲▲▲▲▲▲▲▲▲▲▲▲▲▲

In MEXICO, rice is served as a separate course – *sopa seca* (dry soup), normally after *sopa aguada* (watery soup). However, outside Mexico it is more often served as a side-dish. Mexican rice can be mixed with anything from beans, chillies, carrots, peas and corn to chicken, fish and shellfish, to give it flavour and colour and sometimes to convert it into an all in one dish. Rice and beans feature in almost every menu, either separately or together. Because Mexicans fry their rice before steaming it, it lends itself to freezing and reheating without losing either flavour or texture. It also reheats well in microwave ovens and I find it to be the most tasty rice I have ever tried.

I have included egg dishes in this chapter because, like rice, they can become a light meal, in fact I often prepare these egg dishes as a light lunch. Eggs couple so well with the Mexican *tortillas*, beans and *salsas*, and are used in Mexico for brunch or supper. They are often prepared in a different way each day.

Arroz Blanco

PLAIN WHITE RICE

SERVES 4

This recipe will make rice that is tasty enough to be served on its own, but can also be used for any recipe calling for plain cooked rice. A favourite of mine is rice with fresh banana sliced on to it at the table, that is when fried plantain is not available! Slices of avocado or *guacamole* are also great companions for any rice dish. If you use American 'Easy-Cook' rice, you can be sure the grains will separate easily. Brown rice takes longer to cook but the same recipe can be followed, adding a little more water. For extra colour and heat, finely chopped red chilli can be stirred into the cooked rice before serving.

INGREDIENTS

2 tablespoons oil	2 sprigs fresh parsley or coriander
1 clove garlic	¹/₂ onion, finely chopped
175 g (6 oz) long-grain rice	1 green chilli
450 ml (³/₄ pint) boiling water	
¹/₂ teaspoon salt or 1 chicken stock cube, crumbled	

METHOD

■ Heat the oil in a heavy-based saucepan with a tight-fitting lid, and fry the garlic clove until it becomes black. Add the rice, and fry for about 4 minutes, stirring occasionally, until the rice loses its stickiness and becomes easier to stir and white instead of translucent, but do not fry until golden. Remove the garlic from the pan and drain off any excess oil.

■ Add the water and all the remaining ingredients to the rice and bring quickly to the boil while you are watching it. Reduce the heat to a slow simmer, cover and cook for 15 minutes. When ready, there should be no water left in the bottom of the pan, and the rice should have doubled in volume and become light and fluffy. Remove and discard the herbs and chilli. Serve hot or cold.

Arroz Poblano

RICE CASSEROLE WITH PEPPERS, CREAM AND CHEESE

SERVES 8

This is a proven success, suitable for buffet dinners. It is an attractive and tasty dish and quite unique; I haven't come across other recipes that use rice and cheese together in quite the same way. For vegetarian meals, corn kernels, peas and carrots add to its originality. The casserole freezes well; or it can be prepared ahead of time and refrigerated, then baked when required. It also reheats well in the microwave.

INGREDIENTS

150 ml ('/4 pint) soured cream	2 green chillies, sliced
150 ml ('/4 pint) single cream	2 green peppers, deseeded and sliced
'/2 teaspoon salt	1 red pepper, deseeded and sliced
'/4 teaspoon black pepper	50 g (2 oz) cooked corn kernels (optional)
75 g (3 oz) Cheddar cheese, grated	50 g (2 oz) cooked peas (optional)
75 g (3 oz) mozzarella cheese, grated	2 carrots, diced and cooked (optional)
1 quantity cooked *Arroz Blanco* (see page 98)	

METHOD

■ Lightly grease a 25 × 18 cm (10 × 7 inch) ovenproof dish. Mix the creams with the salt and pepper, and blend the cheeses together. Layer the cooked rice, chillies, peppers, vegetables (if using), cream and cheese in the dish, finishing with cheese. Bake in the top of the oven at 180°C, 350°F, Gas Mark 4 for about 30 minutes or until the cheese browns and the rice around the edges looks dry.

Arroz con Camarón Seco

RICE AND DRIED SHRIMPS

SERVES 6

This is a very flavourful rice dish. Dried shrimps can be bought from any Chinese grocer.

INGREDIENTS

100 g (4 oz) dried shrimps	2 tablespoons chopped fresh parsley
450 ml (³/₄ pint) water	¹/₂ onion, finely chopped
2 tablespoons corn oil	¹/₂ teaspoon salt
1 clove garlic	2 green chillies, finely sliced
175 g (6 oz) long-grain rice	2 tablespoons tomato purée

METHOD

■ Rinse the shrimps in a sieve under cold running water, then put them in a saucepan with the 450 ml (³/₄ pint) water. Boil for 5 minutes, then drain and reserve all the liquid. Ensure all the shrimps are peeled and remove any skin, heads or whiskers.

■ Heat the oil in a large heavy-based frying pan with a tight-fitting lid. Fry the garlic clove until black, then add the rice and fry, stirring constantly, until the rice is golden. Drain off excess oil and discard the garlic.

■ Add the cooked shrimps and the rest of the ingredients to the rice. Stir once, bring quickly to the boil, then lower the heat to a simmer, cover and cook for 20–25 minutes.

VARIATION

MEXICAN ARROZ CON JITOMATE Simply omit the dried shrimps from the above recipe.

Moros con Cristianos

—————— RICE AND BLACK BEANS WITH FRIED PLANTAIN ——————

▲▲▲

SERVES 6

Most dishes that include plantain are associated with Tabasco (in south-east Mexico) or the Gulf of Mexico. This combination is popular in Cuba, Mexico and some other Latin countries. It is often served with fried eggs and garnished with hot tomato sauce, making it a complete meal. The combination of beans and rice makes this a very nutritious dish.

INGREDIENTS

2 tablespoons oil	½ onion, finely chopped
1 clove garlic	2 green chillies, chopped
175 g (6 oz) long-grain rice	150 g (5 oz) cooked black beans (see page 28)
2 tablespoons tomato purée	
1 chicken stock cube, crumbled	450 ml (¾ pint) boiling water
2 tablespoons chopped fresh parsley	2 ripe plantains

METHOD

■ Heat the oil in a saucepan with a tight-fitting lid and fry the garlic clove until it turns black. Discard the garlic and add the rice to the pan. Fry, stirring constantly, until the rice is an even golden colour. (This process is important to stop the rice going mushy.) Drain off as much oil as possible and reserve.

■ Add all the remaining ingredients, except the plantains, to the rice and bring to the boil. Reduce the heat, cover and simmer gently for 20–25 minutes or until all the liquid has been absorbed.

■ Meanwhile, put the plantains on the work surface and roll them with the palms of your hands as if they were rolling pins. This softens the flesh and makes them sweet. Cut the skins lengthways with a sharp knife, and peel them off and reserve. Cut the plantains in half and then cut each half into four long slices. Heat the reserved oil in a frying pan, and fry the plantain slices over medium heat until golden on both sides. Keep warm in their skins. When the rice is ready, transfer it to a serving dish and arrange the fried plantain on top.

VARIATION

Top each portion with a fried egg and hot *Salsa de Jitomate* (page 35).

Machaca con Huevo

──────── SCRAMBLED EGGS WITH JERKY ────────

SERVES 4

Machaca con Huevo and *Huevos con Cecina* are the same dish. The word *machaca* is used because after the meat is dried it is pounded (*machacar*) to break it up into small strands which are easier to chew. This dried meat (*cecina*) is particularly good cooked with scrambled eggs and wrapped in a flour *tortilla*. In rural areas of Mexico, the peons carry their lunch in *itacates* (little parcels) containing a few *burritos* filled with beans and *Machaca con Huevo* or any other filling available. It also makes a good breakfast, brunch or easy supper dish. *Pemican* or *biltong* (jerky), or any other type of dried meat, make good substitutes.

INGREDIENTS

225 g (8 oz) *cecina*	pinch of ground black pepper
3 tablespoons oil	2 green chillies, sliced
2 ripe tomatoes, quartered	8 eggs, beaten
¹/₂ onion, finely chopped	8 warm wheat flour *tortillas* (see page 26)
¹/₄ teaspoon salt	

METHOD

■ If you are using fresh *cecina*, grill it on both sides until it looks very dry. Place it on absorbent kitchen paper and break it up into very small pieces, pounding it with the back of a knife if necessary.

■ Heat the oil in a non-stick frying pan and fry the *cecina* for 5–6 minutes or until it is brown and very crisp. Add the tomatoes, onion, salt and pepper to the pan and fry for about 3 minutes, stirring occasionally, until the tomato is partially cooked. Add the chillies and eggs and cook for a few minutes, stirring occasionally, to ensure the egg is cooked evenly. Spoon some mixture on to each warm flour *tortilla*, roll it over the mixture and fold the edges in. Keep the *burritos* warm inside a folded tea-towel. Serve hot with refried beans (see page 31).

Huevos Revueltos con Chorizo

SCRAMBLED EGGS WITH SPICY SAUSAGE

SERVES 4

This egg dish reminds me of my life in Mexico. Sometimes for breakfast I used to fill a warm French-style miniature loaf, called *bolillo*, with *Huevos con Chorizo* and have it with black beans and *epazote*.

INGREDIENTS

3 tablespoons oil	$^{1}/_{4}$ teaspoon salt
225 g (8 oz) chorizo, sliced if bought	pinch of ground black pepper
3 firm ripe tomatoes, quartered	3 green chillies, sliced
$^{1}/_{2}$ onion, finely chopped	6 eggs, well beaten

METHOD

■ Heat the oil in a non-stick frying pan and fry the *chorizo* for about 3 minutes, stirring continually, then remove it from the pan. Add the tomatoes, onion, salt and pepper to the pan and fry for about 3 minutes or until the tomato is partially cooked. Add the chillies, *chorizo* and beaten eggs and cook for a few minutes, stirring occasionally, to ensure the egg cooks evenly. Slide the mixture on to a warm plate, and serve immediately.

Huevos Rancheros

—— FRIED EGGS WITH BEANS, *TORTILLA* AND TOMATO SAUCE ——

SERVES 6

This is by far my favourite way of eating fried eggs. In most Mexican restaurants *Huevos Rancheros* are served on a soft *tortilla* which has been flash-fried, but I prefer to use a crisp *tortilla* which adds texture to the already delicious dish. In Mexico, this is served as a brunch or lunch dish, but I often have it for supper. Garnishes vary from crumbled cheese to sliced avocado. Serve it with warm French bread to mop up the sauce. Remember, you need to have the sauce made, the beans refried and the *tortillas* fried before you start frying the eggs, which should be eaten immediately. I'm afraid, for this recipe, 'frying pan to table' is a must.

INGREDIENTS

6 tablespoons oil	12 eggs
12 corn *tortillas* (see page 24)	GARNISH
1 quantity *Salsa para Enchiladas* (see page 35)	100 g (4 oz) Cheddar cheese, grated
	1 ripe avocado, sliced just before serving
150 g (5 oz) *Frijoles Refritos* of spreading texture (see page 31)	3 green chillies, sliced

METHOD

■ Heat the oil in a frying pan and fry the *tortillas* until they are crisp and golden brown. Drain on absorbent kitchen paper. Remove the pan from the heat and drain off most of the oil, reserving just enough to fry the eggs.

■ In separate saucepans (or in a microwave), heat the sauce and the beans. Spread the beans on the *tortillas* and place two *tortillas* on each of six plates, slightly overlapping. (Alternatively, serve the beans on the side). Heat the remaining oil in the frying pan and fry two eggs at a time. Place the eggs immediately on top of the *tortillas* on one plate, cover with sauce and top with your choice of garnish (or all three garnishes). Serve at once. Repeat until all the eggs are fried.

Nopales con Huevo

PADDLE CACTUS WITH SCRAMBLED EGGS

SERVES 4

This unusual breakfast dish goes extremely well with *Frijoles Negros* (cooked black beans, see page 28) and warm *tortillas*.

INGREDIENTS

4 tablespoons oil

6 eggs

1 tablespoon water

4 spring onions, finely chopped

2 green chillies, finely chopped

225 g (8 oz) canned or precooked *nopales* (see page 20)

pinch of salt

$^1/_4$ teaspoon ground black pepper

METHOD

■ Heat the oil in an omelette pan or small frying pan over moderate heat. Beat the eggs well with the water and add to the pan with all the other ingredients. Stir with a wooden spatula, carefully tilting the frying pan to ensure all the *nopales* are covered in egg and the egg is cooked. Serve at once.

Rosca de Arroz con Camarones en Adobo

—————— RICE RING WITH PRAWNS IN RED CHILLI SAUCE ——————

SERVES 4

This hot rice ring is tasty and colourful, featuring, as so many other Mexican dishes do, the green, white and red of the national flag. Serve it as a main course along with salad and *Esquites* (see page 166).

INGREDIENTS

1 kg (2 lb) fresh uncooked prawns	2 sprigs fresh parsley
900 ml (1½ pints) water	1 onion, finely chopped
1 teaspoon salt	2 green chillies
2 tablespoons oil	1 quantity *Salsa Adobada* (see page 36)
1 clove garlic	½ lettuce, finely shredded
175 g (6 oz) long-grain rice	

METHOD

■ Rinse the prawns in a sieve under cold running water. Put the 900 ml (1½ pints) water in a saucepan and bring to the boil. Add the salt, then add the prawns and simmer, uncovered, for 5 minutes. Remove from the heat and drain, reserving the liquid. Shell and devein the prawns.

■ Heat the oil in a heavy-based saucepan with a tight-fitting lid and fry the garlic clove until black. Discard the garlic and add the rice to the pan. Fry for about 4 minutes, stirring, until it has changed colour. Drain off all the excess oil and add 450 ml (¾ pint) of the reserved prawn liquid. Stir in the parsley, onion and chillies. Cover and bring to the boil, then reduce the heat and simmer for 15 minutes, or until all the liquid is absorbed. The rice will double in volume and become fluffy. Discard the parsley and chillies.

■ Bring the *Salsa Adobada* to the boil, add the prawns and cook for 2 minutes. While the rice is still hot, put it in a greased 23 cm (9 inch) ring mould, pressing down firmly. Invert the mould on to a serving dish, spoon the prawns and sauce into the centre, and decorate the ring with more prawns. Surround the ring with shredded lettuce.

VARIATIONS

Fill the centre of the ring with any other filling you choose – meat, chicken or vegetables. *Salsa de Jitomate Típica* (see page 34) makes an attractive alternative centre if you wish to keep the meal simple.

Arroz con Pollo

RICE WITH CHICKEN

SERVES 8

This is very similar to an Italian risotto or Spanish paella. It is one of the most popular rice dishes in Latin America and the Caribbean. Fish, mussels, prawns or cooked pork are good substitutes for the chicken or can be added to it. This is an all-in-one meal, suitable for a large crowd; excellent for teenagers' lunches. Serve with a tossed salad and sliced avocado.

INGREDIENTS

4 chicken portions, cut into large pieces	2 tablespoons tomato purée
juice of 1 lemon	50 g (2 oz) corn kernels
$^1/_2$ teaspoon ground black pepper	50 g (2 oz) carrots, diced
$^1/_2$ teaspoon salt	50 g (2 oz) peas
2 cloves garlic, crushed	50 g (2 oz) cabbage, shredded
4 tablespoons oil	50 g (2 oz) runner beans, sliced
150 ml ($^1/_4$ pint) water	2 sticks celery, sliced
2 onions, finely chopped	2 medium potatoes, peeled and cut into 1 cm ($^1/_2$ inch) cubes
175 g (6 oz) long-grain rice	1 red pepper, deseeded and cut into strips
450 ml ($^3/_4$ pint) boiling water	4 miniature globe artichokes, cut lengthways in half (optional)
4 green chillies	
4 sprigs fresh parsley, finely chopped	

METHOD

■ Season the chicken pieces with lemon juice, pepper, salt and garlic. Heat the oil in a frying pan, and fry the chicken on all sides until golden. Drain off all the oil and reserve. Add half the water and all onions to the pan, cover and simmer for about 30 minutes, basting frequently, until the chicken is just tender. Drain, reserving any juices. Discard all skin and bones.

■ Heat the reserved oil in a large heavy-based frying pan with a tight-fitting lid. Add the rice and fry, stirring, until golden. Drain off excess oil. Add the cooked chicken meat and all the remaining ingredients to the rice.

■ Measure the reserved chicken juices and top up with boiling water to make 450 ml ($^3/_4$ pint). Add to the rice mixture, stir and bring to the boil quickly. Lower the heat, cover and simmer for 25–30 minutes or until all the water has been absorbed. (Rice must never boil briskly or it will stick.) Remove the chillies, if preferred, and serve hot.

FISH

▲▲▲▲▲▲▲▲▲▲▲▲▲▲▲▲▲

MEXICO is surrounded by 6,300 miles of coastline, which provides an abundance of fish and seafood. The Gulf of Mexico, the Caribbean Sea, the Gulf of Cortés and the Pacific Ocean all contribute, and a number of freshwater fish are also available.

Such a variety of fresh fish provides unequalled opportunities for the Mexican menu. Red snapper, snapper, flounder, mackerel, bass, tuna, albacore, swordfish and sole are amongst the more popular types of fish available. In the San Juan fish market in Mexico City, a banner proudly advertises: 'The fish that you buy here today slept in the sea last night'! Freshwater varieties include rainbow trout, perch, *blanco de Patzcuaro* as well as many others from the lakes and rivers. Other seafood includes turtle, squid, clams, abalone, conch, oysters, mussels, crayfish, lobster, prawns, crabs and king crabs.

Two of the most popular dishes in the Mexican repertoire are *Huachinango a la Veracruzana* and *Seviche* (sometimes spelled *Ceviche*). Both dishes are traditionally prepared with red snapper, but cod or haddock are good substitutes. Although fresh fish is abundant in Mexico, a number of popular recipes, originally introduced by the Spaniards, call for dried fish, such as *Bacalao a la Vizcaina* and *Arroz con Camarón Seco*.

Methods of preparing fish in Mexico are very varied. Grilling and frying are done in much the same way as in Europe. Lime or lemon is always used to season fish and also as a garnish, with the occasional dash of Worcestershire sauce. Any of the wide variety of sauces can be used to prepare succulent fish dishes. The *Pibil* style of cooking from Yucatán also appears to be a favourite with fish.

Seviche

LIME MARINATED FISH WITH FRESH CORIANDER

SERVES 4

This deservedly popular dish originally came from Polynesia. It is one dish that Mexico shares with the rest of its South American neighbours, though methods of preparing it are endlessly varied.

The fish is 'cooked', as it were, in the acid of the lime. The fish pieces must therefore be small to allow the lime to penetrate. Marinating overnight is essential for best results. Prawns, sliced lobster tails, cod, haddock, mackerel, monkfish, bass, salmon or scallops may replace the traditional red snapper. It will keep in the refrigerator for up to 2 days after it has been fully assembled.

Seviche makes a useful starter served in a cocktail cup or as a filling for half an avocado. Alternatively, serve it on a bed of lettuce for a light lunch. For canapés, place the cubed fish on cocktail sticks and make miniature kebabs with cubed tomato, green pepper, half an olive and a caper. Marinate for 18 hours, then drain, season and garnish with finely chopped coriander.

INGREDIENTS

225 g (8 oz) fish fillets, skinned, boned and cut into bite-sized cubes	¼ teaspoon dried oregano
juice of 1 orange	¼ teaspoon salt
juice of 3 limes	¼ teaspoon ground black pepper
6 spring onions, thinly sliced	2 ripe tomatoes, finely chopped
2 tablespoons tomato ketchup	8 sprigs fresh coriander, finely chopped
½ teaspoon Worcestershire sauce	1 green chilli, finely chopped
dash of Tabasco sauce	2 ripe avocados (optional)

METHOD

■ Place the fish in a non-metallic container, pour the citrus juices over it and mix in the spring onions. Cover, refrigerate and leave overnight. The fish will become very white instead of translucent, and the juices will become milky.

■ Add all the remaining ingredients, except the avocados, to the fish, stir and marinate until required. Before serving, cut the avocados in half, remove the stones and fill with *seviche*. Carefully spoon some of the marinade over the top and serve on a bed of lettuce.

Bacalao a la Vizcaina

SALT COD WITH OLIVES AND NEW POTATOES

SERVES 6

This rich main course needs preparing a day in advance. *Bacalao* is a dish of Spanish origin and is considered a delicacy. It makes a delicious filling for *Empanaditas* (see opposite). *Bacalao* (salt cod) is easy to purchase from Italian or West Indian shops as well as from larger fishmongers.

INGREDIENTS

275 g (10 oz) salted cod (*bacalao*)	15 stuffed green olives, sliced
225 g (8 oz) small new potatoes	4 tablespoons tomato purée
40 g (1¹/₂ oz) butter	¹/₄ teaspoon dried oregano
¹/₂ onion, finely sliced	¹/₄ teaspoon sugar
1 red pepper, deseeded and thinly sliced	

METHOD

■ Cover the fish with cold water and leave to soak overnight. Drain, transfer to a saucepan, cover with fresh water and simmer for 15 minutes. Drain again, cover with more water for a third time, and simmer for a further 25 minutes. Drain and cool.

■ Meanwhile, cook the new potatoes in boiling salted water for about 15 minutes. Drain, reserving the cooking water, and cool. Cut the potatoes into quarters.

■ Use your fingers to shred the fish as finely as possible, searching for bones as you go. Heat the butter in a frying pan and sauté the onion and pepper until soft. Add the fish and 250 ml (8 fl oz) potato cooking water with all the remaining ingredients, mixing well. Cover and simmer for about 5 minutes or until the mixture starts to become dry. Serve hot with rice, a mixed salad and crispy white bread rolls.

Empanada de Bacalao

---- SALT COD TURNOVER ----

SERVES 6

This is an unusual turnover because of its size and filling. It looks a treat and tastes delicious. It is ideal for a buffet table and can be made into individual cocktail-size *empanaditas* if preferred.

INGREDIENTS

1 quantity Rough Puff Pastry (see page 41)	1 egg, lightly beaten
1 quantity cold *Bacalao a la Vizcaina* (see opposite)	

METHOD

■ Roll out the pastry on a lightly floured surface to a large rectangle 3 mm ($^1/_8$ inch) thick. Place on a greased baking tray, spoon the *balacao* mixture on one half, brush the pastry edges with a little water, and fold over the other half of the pastry to cover the filling. Seal the edges by pressing with a fork, and prick the pastry all over. Brush with beaten egg and bake in the oven at 220°C, 425°F, Gas Mark 7 for about 15 minutes or until golden. Cool on a wire rack for about 20 minutes or serve hot.

VARIATION

For individual miniature *empanadas*, cut the pastry into rounds with a 7.5 cm (3 inch) cutter. Fill one half of each round with *bacalao*, brush the pastry edges with a little water, fold over and press to seal. Pierce the tops with a fork, brush with egg and place on a greased baking tray. Bake as above and serve warm.

Jaibas al Horno

BAKED CRAB

SERVES 4

This excellent starter is sure to impress. It is often prepared as a treat in our house as my youngest daughter, Elena, requests it for any special occasion. It need not be an expensive dish to make because you can use canned white crab meat. It is especially attractive if baked in the crab shells, which can be washed and re-used, or in scallop shells which you can buy from your fishmonger.

INGREDIENTS

175 g (6 oz) white crab meat (fresh, frozen or canned)

50 g (2 oz) butter

6 spring onions, finely chopped

6 sprigs fresh parsley, finely chopped

1/4 teaspoon Tabasco sauce

1 teaspoon Worcestershire sauce

1/2 chicken stock cube, crumbled

1/4 teaspoon ground black pepper

1 tablespoon tomato purée

50 g (2 oz) fine breadcrumbs

4 slices lemon

4 sprigs fresh parsley

METHOD

■ If you are using live crab, plunge it into boiling water for 10 minutes. Crack open the shell and carefully pick all the white meat from the shell and claws. If using frozen or canned crab meat, drain it carefully and search for and remove any small bones and pieces of shell.

■ Melt the butter in a frying pan, and sauté the onions and chopped parsley for about 3 minutes, stirring constantly. Add the crab meat and all the remaining ingredients, except the breadcrumbs, lemon slices and parsley sprigs, and fry gently, stirring occasionally. When the mixture starts to dry out, spoon it into individual ovenproof dishes or well-scrubbed and buttered shells. Place them on a baking tray and cook in the oven at 180°C, 350°F, Gas Mark 4 for about 15 minutes. Sprinkle over the breadcrumbs and return to the oven for another 10 minutes or until lightly browned on top. Serve hot, garnished with lemon slices and parsley.

OPPOSITE   Clockwise from top: *Totopos* (corn tortilla chips, page 46), *Seviche* (lime-marinated prawns, salmon and scallops with fresh coriander, page 109), *Empanadas de Bacalao* (miniature salt cod turnovers, page 111), *Salsa de Jitomate Típica* (uncooked tomato sauce, page 34) and *Cocktail de Tequila* (Tequila sunrise, page 199)

OVERLEAF   Top to bottom: *Escabeche Tropical* (prawn and fish escabeche with coconut, page 114) and *Ensalada Navideña* (Christmas salad, page 172)

Huachinango a la Veracruzana

———— COD WITH CAPERS, OLIVES AND SPICES ————

ᐱᐯᐱ

SERVES 4

This is by far the most popular way of eating fish in Mexico. It is traditionally made with a whole red snapper, but cod, haddock or any white fish are equally good. Although a whole fish is more authentic, you might prefer to use fillets, as bones are hard to spot once the sauce is covering the fish. Italian *pepperoni* are long, thin yellow peppers available bottled in England. In Mexico they are known as *chilacas*; their flavour is not very hot. Offer crusty French bread to mop up the tasty sauce.

INGREDIENTS

4 cod or haddock fillets, skinned (see Note)	18 capers
¹/₂ lime or lemon	18 stuffed green olives
¹/₄ teaspoon salt	¹/₄ teaspoon Worcestershire sauce
¹/₄ teaspoon ground black pepper	pinch of dried oregano
450 ml (³/₄ pint) *Salsa para Enchiladas* (see page 35)	1 bay leaf
juice of 1 orange	4 Italian yellow *pepperoni*, drained
1 red pepper, deseeded and sliced	chopped fresh parsley and orange slices, to garnish
¹/₂ onion, finely sliced	

METHOD

■ Rub the fish with the lime, squeezing the juice as you go. Sprinkle with salt and pepper and leave to marinate for 30 minutes. Put the fish in a greased ovenproof dish and add the *Salsa*, orange juice, red pepper, onion, capers, olives, Worcestershire sauce, oregano, bay leaf and *pepperoni*. Cover and bake in the oven at 180°C, 350°F, Gas Mark 4 for about 40 minutes. When cooked, the fish flesh should separate easily. Uncover and continue baking for another 15 minutes to reduce the juices, basting frequently. Serve hot, garnished with parsley and orange slices.

NOTE If you are using a whole fish, ask the fishmonger to descale it for you. Wash it well on the outside, rinse the inside, then rub it with the lime. If you are using cod fillets, skin them by holding on to the tail end and placing a sharp knife at an angle between the flesh and the skin. Work the knife against the skin whilst you pull gently. If the fish is too slippery to hold, rub some salt on it to give you a grip, but wash it off afterwards. Remove all the bones you can find, and cut off the bony section in the thick-fleshed end of each fillet.

Escabeche Tropical

PRAWN AND FISH *ESCABECHE* WITH COCONUT

SERVES 6

This unusual fish dish is suitable for a party. If you wish to create a special effect, serve the *Escabeche* on coconut halves or hollowed out pineapple halves.

INGREDIENTS

175 g (6 oz) white crab meat (fresh, canned or frozen)	4 large tomatoes, peeled and chopped
30 large uncooked prawns, peeled	8 sprigs fresh coriander, finely chopped
1 cod fillet, skinned and cubed	4 green chillies, sliced
1/2 teaspoon salt	125 g (4 oz) unsweetened shredded coconut
1/2 teaspoon ground black pepper	100 ml (4 fl oz) dry white wine
juice of 1 lemon	4 dashes Tabasco sauce
3 tablespoons olive oil	4 dashes Worcestershire sauce
2 carrots, cut into thin strips	2 tablespoons tomato ketchup
1 small onion, thinly sliced	1/2 teaspoon dried oregano

METHOD

■ Mix together the crab meat, prawns and fish, and season with the salt, black pepper and lemon juice. Heat the olive oil in a heavy-based frying pan and sauté the fish mixture for about 8 minutes, stirring continually. Remove the fish from the pan with a slotted spoon. Add the carrots, onion, tomatoes, coriander, chillies and coconut to the oil remaining in the pan and sauté until soft. Add the wine, Tabasco, Worcestershire sauce and ketchup. Sprinkle with oregano and simmer gently. Remove from the heat. Mix in the fish, cool and refrigerate. Serve cold.

Camarones a la Mexicana

PRAWNS IN TOMATILLO SAUCE

SERVES 4

This is a delicious combination that goes well with white rice and warm *tortillas*. It can be served hot or cold; if tomatilloes are not available, use *Salsa para Enchiladas*.

INGREDIENTS

1 quantity *Salsa de Tomate Verde* (see page 33) or *Salsa para Enchiladas* (see page 35)

24 large uncooked prawns, peeled

1 tablespoon fresh parsley, chopped

1 chilli, sliced

pinch of salt

pinch of ground black pepper

2 dashes Worcestershire sauce

juice of ½ lemon

lemon slices, to garnish

METHOD

■ Bring the *Salsa* to the boil, add the prawns and simmer for 7 minutes. Add the parsley, chilli, salt, black pepper, Worcestershire sauce and lemon juice, and simmer for a further 5 minutes. Serve hot or cold, garnished with lemon slices.

Tortitas De Camarón Seco

DRIED SHRIMP FRITTERS

SERVES 6

These fritters are used for vigil festivities like Easter and Christmas. For the latter they are served with *Romeritos*, also known as *Revoltijo*. *Romeritos* is a green leafy vegetable that grows well around that season. It is usually stewed in *mole* sauce, but also goes well with any other type of *salsa*. Finely shredded spinach is a good substitute.

INGREDIENTS

450 g (1 lb) dried shrimps, peeled and heads and tails removed

100 g (4 oz) breadcrumbs

2 large eggs, separated

oil

METHOD

■ Cook the shrimps in boiling water for about 15 minutes, then drain. Save some whole shrimps for garnish and put the rest in a food processor with the breadcrumbs. Process to a coarse paste.

■ Whisk the egg whites until stiff. In a separate bowl, beat egg yolks until they are pale. Blend the yolks with the whites, then add the shrimp mixture. Heat the oil in a frying pan, and fry the shrimp batter, 1 tablespoon at a time, on medium heat, until golden. Drain on absorbent kitchen paper and add to any hot boiling *salsa* just before serving.

Seviche de Camarónes

MARINATED PRAWNS

SERVES 6

For *Seviche* (or *Ceviche*) the fish or shellfish are 'cooked' in the acid from the lime juice. This recipe uses prawns, which must be bought raw, then peeled and cut into five before using.

INGREDIENTS

1 kg (2 lb) uncooked prawns, peeled, washed and chopped	18 stuffed olives, cut in half
juice of 6 limes	100 ml (4 fl oz) olive oil
3 spring onions, finely chopped	4 tablespoons tomato ketchup
2 tomatoes, finely chopped	$\frac{1}{2}$ teaspoon Worcestershire sauce
4 sprigs fresh coriander, finely chopped	$\frac{1}{4}$ teaspoon Tabasco sauce
1 green chilli, very finely chopped	$\frac{1}{4}$ teaspoon salt
$\frac{1}{2}$ teaspoon chopped fresh oregano	$\frac{1}{4}$ teaspoon ground black pepper
$\frac{1}{2}$ teaspoon chopped fresh thyme	2 ripe avocados
	$\frac{1}{2}$ small lettuce, finely shredded

METHOD

■ Put the prawns in a non-metallic dish with the lime juice and spring onions. Stir to coat, then leave to marinate for at least 4 hours. Mix together all the remaining ingredients, except the avocados and lettuce. When the prawns' flesh is white and no longer transparent, mix the ingredients into the marinade. Cut the avocados in half, remove the stones and fill the avocado halves with the prawns, spooning some juice over them. Serve the avocados on a bed of lettuce, accompanied by crackers.

Pescado al Arriero

—— COD FILLETS IN WHITE SAUCE WITH PEPPERS ——

SERVES 4

This dish is very quick to prepare and makes a good main course with potatoes, boiled peas and sweetcorn. Any type of fish can be used.

INGREDIENTS

4 fillets of fish, skinned	250 ml (8 fl oz) evaporated milk
¹/₂ lemon	¹/₂ chicken stock cube, crumbled
¹/₄ teaspoon salt	2 bay leaves
¹/₄ teaspoon ground black pepper	2 green chillies, sliced
2 tablespoons plain flour	pinch of grated nutmeg
50 g (2 oz) butter	dash of Worcestershire sauce
¹/₂ onion, sliced	sprigs of parsley, to garnish
1 *Poblano* chilli or 1 green pepper, deseeded and finely sliced	

METHOD

■ Dry the fish with absorbent kitchen paper and rub with the lemon half, squeezing the juice over the fillets. Sprinkle with salt and pepper, and dip each fillet in flour. Heat the butter in a heavy-based frying pan and sauté the onion and chilli or pepper until soft. Add the fish and all the remaining ingredients, except the parsley sprigs. Spoon over the liquid, cover and simmer over low heat for 20 minutes, stirring occasionally to prevent sticking. Alternatively, transfer to an ovenproof dish, cover and bake in the oven at 180°C, 350°F, Gas Mark 4 for 30 minutes. Garnish with sprigs of parsley.

POULTRY

▲▲▲▲▲▲▲▲▲▲▲▲▲▲▲▲

CHICKENS were introduced to the New World by the Spaniards. Chicken meat and eggs soon became popular and a complete range of new dishes appeared. Today, chicken is as popular in Mexico as it is in Britain, and is often used instead of pork.

Some restaurants specialise in roasting chicken slowly over a wood fire; the enticing smell and country atmosphere attract customers. Roast chicken is also popular take-away food, accompanied by potato crisps made by the restaurant. The Mexican touch comes from the *jalapeño* chillies used, which add a distinctive flavour to the juicy wood-roasted chicken. When chicken is boiled, the stock is used for *caldo*, the liver and giblets to flavour rice, and the meat becomes a filling for *tacos* or *fajitas* as well as being used in composite dishes like *Budín Azteca*. Chicken roasted in the traditional British way is equally good as a filling for soft, warm *tortillas* accompanied by *salsa* and *guacamole*.

Turkey had already been domesticated by the Aztecs by the time the Spaniards arrived. The Aztecs also ate wild duck and pheasant. Of the three, turkey remains the most popular in Mexico today, probably because it features in the national dish, *Mole Poblano* or *Molli* (which means sauce). Turkey's healthy image is gaining it more popularity; it can be used in any recipe calling for pork or chicken.

Duck dishes are quite rare in modern Mexico. They are found on restaurant menus but duck is not often cooked at home. Pheasant features in the diet of southern Mexico, where deer, turtle and iguana meat are also eaten.

Taquitos de Pollo

CRISPY CHICKEN *TORTILLA* ROLLS

SERVES 6

*T*aquitos de Pollo are the most popular way of eating *tortillas*. They could also be considered *antojitos* as they can be offered as a snack, a starter or a main course, depending on the amount you serve per person. *Taquitos* are usually served garnished with *guacamole* and accompanied by refried beans, salad and rice. They are very crispy and can be eaten as finger-food.

INGREDIENTS

oil	1 quantity *Guacamole* (see page 48)
18 corn *tortillas* (see page 24)	1 lettuce, very finely chopped, to serve
3 cooked chicken breasts, skinned and shredded	

METHOD

■ Heat about 2.5 cm (1 inch) oil in a deep frying pan. Flash-fry the *tortillas* for no longer than 3 seconds, and stack them on absorbent kitchen paper as they are done. While the *tortillas* are still warm, place a piece of cooked chicken in the middle of a *tortilla* and roll it tightly. Repeat until all the *tortillas* are filled. (At this stage, you can either refrigerate or freeze the *Taquitos* in a sealed container).

■ Before serving, either refry the *Taquitos* in shallow oil until golden and crisp, or place them on a baking tray uncovered in the oven at 190°C, 375°C, Gas Mark 5 for 15 minutes. Spread a little *Guacamole* along the length of each *Taquito* and arrange them on a bed of finely chopped lettuce.

Pollo en Salsa de Chilpotle

CHICKEN IN SMOKED *JALAPEÑO* SAUCE

SERVES 4

Chilpotle (dried smoked *jalapeño*) chillies are very popular throughout Mexico and their smoky flavour is delightful. If *chilpotles* are not available, you could try any of the other Mexican dried chillies, or, as a last resort, you could substitute 4 tablespoons paprika plus 1 tablespoon cayenne pepper for the chillies. Serve with rice, beans and vegetables of your choice. Preparation should start 3 hours in advance.

INGREDIENTS

6 *chilpotle* or other dried chillies	50 g (2 oz) butter
450 ml (³/₄ pint) boiling water	100 g (4 oz) button mushrooms
4 chicken portions, skinned	2 chicken stock cubes, crumbled
2 tablespoons malt vinegar	¹/₂ onion, roughly chopped
¹/₂ teaspoon salt	2 cloves garlic
¹/₄ teaspoon ground black pepper	150 ml (¹/₄ pint) soured cream

METHOD

■ Heat the chillies in a dry frying pan until pliable. Remove the stems and seeds, and put the chillies in a bowl. Cover with the boiling water and leave to soak for 1 hour. Season the chicken with the vinegar, salt and pepper, and leave to marinate for 30 minutes.

■ Heat the butter in a heavy-based frying pan and fry the chicken until golden on all sides. Remove from the pan and place in an ovenproof casserole.

■ Place half the mushrooms, the stock cubes, onion, garlic, chillies and their soaking water in a blender and blend to a fine paste. Rub through a sieve into the casserole with the chicken. Finely slice the reserved mushrooms and add to the casserole. Cover and cook in the oven at 180°C, 350°F, Gas Mark 4 for about 1¹/₂ hours or until the chicken is very tender. Place the chicken on a warm serving dish and keep warm.

■ Drain the juices from the casserole into a saucepan. Leave for 15 minutes, then remove any fat from the surface. Just before serving, heat the cooking juices and add the soured cream, stirring all the time and being careful not to let it boil. Pour the cream sauce over the hot chicken and serve.

Budin Azteca

TORTILLA CHICKEN CASSEROLE

SERVES 8

*B*udin *Azteca* and *Enchiladas* are related, the latter being the original dish which is time-consuming to prepare and therefore not too practical for big parties. *Budin Azteca*, on the other hand, is a good buffet dish, liked by all. To describe it simply, I would say it is a Mexican-style lasagne, made with chicken and *tortillas* instead of pasta. Soured cream is commonly used but yoghurt could be used instead. This dish is a good introduction to Mexican food, as it is always popular and can be prepared ahead of time and baked just before serving. It goes well with mixed vegetables, rice, and refried beans.

INGREDIENTS

oil	1 green pepper, deseeded and sliced
12 corn *tortillas* (see page 24)	300 ml (¹/₂ pint) soured cream or strained Greek yoghurt, or a combination of the two
1 quantity *Salsa para Enchiladas* (see page 35)	
3 skinless chicken breast fillets, boiled and shredded	275 g (10 oz) mature Cheddar cheese, grated

METHOD

■ Heat some oil in a frying pan and flash-fry the *tortillas* for 20 seconds on each side. Drain on absorbent kitchen paper and keep warm. Grease a medium-sized ovenproof casserole.

■ Bring the *Salsa* to the boil and spoon 6 tablespoons into the casserole. Cover the sauce with one layer of *tortillas*, add pieces of chicken at random, and arrange green pepper slices and more sauce over them. Spoon on some soured cream and sprinkle with one third of the cheese. Repeat until all the *tortillas*, chicken and green pepper are used up. Top with cheese and spoon any remaining sauce around the edges to ensure the *tortillas* do not dry up. Bake in the centre of the oven at 180°C, 350°F, Gas Mark 4 for 40 minutes. Serve hot.

NOTE If you wish to prepare this dish ahead of time, pre-bake it for 20 minutes, then finish the cooking allowing another 10 minutes.

Mole Poblano

—————— TURKEY IN RICH CHILLI SAUCE ——————

ᐯᐱᐯ

SERVES 10

Also known by its Nahuatl name, *Molli*, this is Mexico's national dish. It is made with boiled turkey portions, a variety of dried chillies, nuts, spices and chocolate. As a result it is extremely rich and is better served at a Sunday midday meal, when there is time for a siesta and an afternoon walk, than for an evening dinner. Though it is a delicious dish, it is unusual in texture and colour and sometimes considered an acquired taste.

Molli is said to have originated at a convent in Puebla when a special banquet was organised for a visiting bishop. The nun in charge of the kitchen was asked to create an unforgettable dish. She created *Molli*, and it was so well received that her dish became famous and cooks up and down the country copied her idea, turning it into the country's national dish.

Although turkey is the most commonly used meat for *Molli*, pork and chicken are equally good. I use turkey portions in the recipe below, but you could substitute chicken, pork or turkey fillets cut into chunks. The usual accompaniments are white rice and beans, with soft warm corn *tortillas*. The dish improves overnight when the spices have had time to blend. It also freezes well and any leftovers may be used for *tortas*, or as a filling for soft *tacos*. Don't be put off by the large number of ingredients needed for this dish; they are mostly spices and as Mexican food gains in popularity, it is getting easier to find ready-made *mole* paste.

INGREDIENTS

2.7 kg (6 lb) turkey portions, skinned	3 tablespoons unsalted peanuts
6 tablespoons vinegar	2 corn *tortillas* (see page 24)
1¹/₂ teaspoons salt	100 g (4 oz) raisins
1 teaspoon ground black pepper	6 tablespoons tomato purée
1 teaspoon sugar	6 peppercorns
6 cloves garlic, charred (see page 43) and crushed	12 cloves
8 *mulato* chillies	¹/₂ teaspoon aniseed
8 *ancho* chillies	13 cm (5 inch) stick cinnamon or ¹/₂ teaspoon ground cinnamon
6 *pasilla* chillies	3 onions, charred (see page 43) and quartered
4 *chilpotle* chillies	2 tablespoons plain chocolate, grated
1.7 litres (3 pints) boiling water	8 tablespoons oil
3 tablespoons sesame seeds	
3 tablespoons blanched almonds	

METHOD

■ Wash and trim the turkey portions and place in a non-metallic container. Sprinkle with the vinegar, salt, pepper, sugar and half the garlic, and leave to marinate overnight, or for at least 4 hours.

■ Heat the chillies in a heavy-based frying pan for about 3 minutes, turning them frequently, until pliable. Remove the stems and seeds. Discard the stems but reserve the seeds in case you wish to make the *Molli* hotter. Soak the chillies in 900 ml (1¹/₂ pints) boiling water for about 1 hour.

■ Roast the sesame seeds, almonds and peanuts in a dry frying pan, tossing over moderate heat for about 5 minutes. Heat the *tortillas* in the same pan for 4 minutes, turning occasionally, until they become dry and brittle. Break the *tortillas* into pieces and combine with the soaked chillies and their liquid, most of the roasted nuts (reserving some for garnish), the remaining garlic and all the remaining ingredients, except the oil. Process in several batches in a blender to a smooth paste.

■ Heat the oil in a flameproof casserole and fry the marinated turkey pieces until light golden. Remove the turkey and set aside. Drain off most of the oil, leaving about 4 tablespoons. Sieve the chilli mixture into the hot oil and fry, stirring continuously, for 5 minutes. Add the turkey pieces and the remaining water and simmer gently, uncovered, for about 1¹/₂ hours, stirring often, until the turkey is tender. Alternatively, cover and cook in the oven at 180°C, 350°F, Gas Mark 4 for about 2 hours, stirring and basting frequently. Serve piping hot, garnished with the reserved nuts.

NOTE The sauce for *Molli* should be quite thick, like thin porridge, covering the back of a spoon. If the dish becomes dry and you have to add water during cooking, add only a little at a time, taking care not to thin the sauce too much.

VARIATION

For an easier, lighter version of the sauce, use *Salsa Adobada* (see page 36).

If you cannot find the varieties of chillies required, use the equivalent amount of whichever dried chillies are available.

Mancha Manteles de Pollo

CHICKEN IN CHILLI SAUCE WITH PINEAPPLE, PEARS AND PLANTAIN

SERVES 4

*M*ancha Manteles (literally, 'tablecloth stainer') is the name given to this dish because any drops on the tablecloth might become unremovable stains! So ensure your clothing is well protected too. This main course dish goes well with rice and beans, accompanied by soft warm corn *tortillas*. Preparation should start 3 hours ahead of time; the dish improves if made a day ahead, refrigerated overnight and then reheated thoroughly.

INGREDIENTS

4 *mulato* chillies	5 cm (2 inch) stick cinnamon
600 ml (1 pint) boiling water	2 cloves garlic, charred (see page 43)
4 chicken breasts, skinned	½ onion, charred and quartered (see page 43)
½ teaspoon salt	
¼ teaspoon ground black pepper	1 ripe plantain or 2 unripe bananas, sliced
2 tablespoons malt vinegar	2 unripe pears, peeled, cored and quartered
3 tablespoons oil	
1 tablespoon sesame seeds	2 pineapple slices (fresh or canned), quartered
2 tablespoons blanched almonds	
400 g (14 oz) can of tomatoes	2 tablespoons granulated sugar

METHOD

■ Warm the chillies in a dry frying pan for about 3 minutes or until soft, turning frequently. Discard the stems and seeds, cover the chillies with 300 ml (½ pint) boiling water, and leave to soak for 1 hour. Season the chicken with the salt, pepper and vinegar, and leave to marinate for 1 hour.

■ Heat the oil in a flameproof casserole, and fry the chicken until golden all over. Remove from the pan and keep warm. Strain all but 1 tablespoon oil out of the casserole.

■ Mix the soaked chillies and their water with the sesame seeds, almonds, tomatoes, cinnamon, garlic and onion, and blend to a smooth paste in a blender. Heat the oil in the casserole and sieve the paste into it. Fry for 3–4 minutes, stirring continually. Add the chicken breasts, plantain and remaining water, and simmer, uncovered, for about 40 minutes or until the chicken is tender, stirring occasionally. Alternatively, cover and cook in the oven at 180°C, 350°F, Gas Mark 4 for about 40 minutes. Add the remaining fruit and sugar, and cook for a further 5 minutes. Serve hot.

Pechugas al Pipián

CHICKEN BREASTS IN TOMATILLO SAUCE WITH PUMPKIN SEEDS

᭴᭴᭴

SERVES 4

Pechugas al Pipián are chicken breasts in a sauce (tomato, *Adobo* or green tomatillo) to which ground pumpkin seeds are added. Though I like pumpkin seeds very much, I am not too fond of the ground paste when added to sauces. To my mind, this makes the dish too rich. For this reason, the ground pumpkin seeds in this recipe are optional. I do, however, like the appearance and flavour of a few roasted pumpkin seeds used to garnish the finished dish.

INGREDIENTS

4 large chicken breasts, skinned	2 green chillies
2 teaspoons vinegar	100 ml (4 fl oz) water
½ teaspoon salt	1 quantity *Salsa de Tomate Verde* (see page 33)
¼ teaspoon black pepper	
2 cloves garlic, crushed	4 courgettes, quartered
pinch of sugar	100 g (4 oz) pumpkin seeds, ground (optional)
4 tablespoons oil	
1 onion, charred (see page 43) and quartered	2 tablespoons whole pumpkin seeds, to garnish
pinch of dried oregano	

METHOD

■ Wash the chicken breasts and pat dry with absorbent kitchen paper. Season with the vinegar, salt and pepper. Rub with the garlic, and sprinkle the sugar all over. Heat the oil in a frying pan with a lid and fry the chicken until golden on all sides. Add the onion, oregano, chillies and half the water and cover tightly. Simmer gently for about 30 minutes, basting frequently and adding more water as required. Turn the breasts to ensure they brown on all sides.

■ Add the *Salsa*, courgettes and ground pumpkin seeds (if using) to the chicken and simmer gently for 20 minutes. Meanwhile, heat a dry frying pan and toss the whole pumpkin seeds in it, stirring continually, for about 4 minutes or until they start popping. Use them to garnish the chicken breasts. Serve hot, with warm *tortillas*.

VARIATIONS

Use pork, duck or pheasant instead of chicken. Replace the *Salsa de Tomate*

Faisán al Achiote

—————— PHEASANT IN ANNATTO SAUCE ——————

SERVES 4

This is a simpler way of cooking with *achiote* (annatto seed paste) than the *Pollo al Pibil* (see page 128). I have to confess that I prefer this quicker version, but time is always important to me so I am all for simplifying methods. The pheasant need not be 'high', but this is a matter of personal preference.

INGREDIENTS

1 kg (2 lb) pheasant	1 onion, charred and roughly sliced (see page 43)
50 g (2 oz) *achiote* or *tandoori* paste	
juice of ¹/₂ grapefruit	4 eating apples, quartered and cored
2 tablespoons malt vinegar	100 ml (4 fl oz) red wine
¹/₂ teaspoon salt	2 tablespoons cornflour
¹/₄ teaspoon ground black pepper	4 tablespoons cold water
1 clove garlic, charred and crushed (see page 43)	

METHOD

■ Wash and dry the pheasant. Mix the *achiote* or *tandoori* paste with the grapefruit juice, vinegar, salt, pepper and garlic. Rub the pheasant generously with the paste, inside and out, and place it in a flameproof casserole with the onion, apples and wine. Cover with a tight-fitting lid and bake in the oven at 170°C, 325°F, Gas Mark 3 for 2¹/₂ hours or until the pheasant is cooked, basting frequently.

■ Remove the pheasant from the casserole and place on a serving dish. Arrange the apples around the pheasant. Mix the cornflour to a paste with cold water and add to the juices in the pan. Bring to the boil, stirring constantly, and use as gravy over the pheasant. Serve with rice and mixed vegetables of your choice.

Pollo a la Tabasqueña

CHICKEN TABASCO

SERVES 6

Tabasco is located in the south of Mexico and enjoys tropical weather, so they use allspice, which grows locally, instead of black pepper, and cloves also come into everyday seasoning. This chicken casserole is quite delightful.

INGREDIENTS

6 chicken portions, skinned	1 red pepper, deseeded and cut into strips
juice of 1 lime	2 tablespoons green olives, sliced
2 tablespoons malt vinegar	2 tablespoons capers, drained
¹/₂ teaspoon salt	2 tablespoons seedless raisins
¹/₂ teaspoon ground allspice	100 g (4 oz) chopped ham
6 tablespoons oil	4 tablespoons flaked almonds
2 medium onions, charred and chopped (see page 43)	2 cloves
4 cloves garlic, charred and finely chopped (see page 43)	¹/₂ teaspoon ground cinnamon
6 medium tomatoes, charred, peeled and chopped (see page 43)	250 ml (8 fl oz) plus 3 tablespoons cold water
	1 tablespoon cornflour

METHOD

■ Season the chicken portions with the lime juice, vinegar, salt and allspice, and leave to marinate for 20 minutes.

■ Heat the oil in a heavy-based frying pan with a tight-fitting lid and fry the chicken portions until golden. Remove the chicken from the pan and fry all the other ingredients, except the water and cornflour for about 5 minutes.

■ Drain off any excess oil and return the chicken to the pan. Add 250 ml (8 fl oz) water, cover and simmer for about 1 hour, turning the chicken pieces frequently.

■ Remove the chicken to a warmed serving dish. Mix the cornflour with 3 tablespoons cold water and stir it into the pan juices. Bring to the boil, stirring constantly, until thickened. Pour over the chicken and serve hot.

Pollo al Pibil

ROAST CHICKEN WITH *ACHIOTE*

SERVES 4

The name of this dish is derived from the traditional Mayan method of cooking known as a *pib*. As for a *barbacoa* (see page 147), a hole is dug in the ground and filled with red hot stones, followed by the meat wrapped in banana leaves. Fortunately, the dish can also be prepared in your own oven simply by wrapping the meat in well-greased greaseproof paper inside a square of kitchen foil. Preparation starts the day before so that you can marinate the chicken. The basic seasoning is *achiote*, a paste made from ground annatto seeds and spices. The seasoning is not at all hot but quite flavourful. Annatto may be found in Indian grocery stores, but their *tandoori* mixture is quite similar and therefore makes a good substitute for *achiote*.

Serve this dish with soft warm *tortillas*, black beans and raw purple onion slices. If you can't find purple onions, the dish will look just as authentic if you soak ordinary white onions in the vinegar from pickled beetroot for 24 hours. Drain, sprinkle with salt and use as garnish.

INGREDIENTS

1 chicken, quartered and skinned	juice of 1 Seville orange or ¹/₂ grapefruit
oil	2 cloves garlic, charred and crushed (see page 43)
1 large purple onion, sliced, to garnish	
MARINADE	¹/₂ teaspoon dried oregano
¹/₂ teaspoon salt	¹/₂ teaspoon ground cumin
¹/₂ teaspoon ground black pepper	4 tablespoons *achiote* or *tandoori* paste
pinch of sugar	

METHOD

■ Mix the marinade ingredients together to a smooth paste. Rub generously over the chicken, cover and leave to marinate for 24 hours, turning occasionally.

■ Wrap each chicken portion in well-oiled greaseproof paper, then in kitchen foil, and place in a baking dish. Bake in the oven at 160°C, 325°F, Gas Mark 3 for 2¹/₂ hours or until the chicken is extremely tender and falling off the bone. Unwrap the chicken just before serving, arrange on a warm serving dish and garnish with onion rings. Serve hot.

VARIATIONS

Pork, venison or fish can also be cooked in this way, and are equally delicious.

MEAT

▲▲▲▲▲▲▲▲▲▲▲▲▲▲▲▲▲▲

TRADITIONALLY, Mexican cuisine is not based around meat or fish to the same extent that cooking is in Europe. However, it is important to remember that in Mexico European-style cooking has become an intrinsic part of the cuisine, and nowadays a chicken or pork roast or fricassee is as at home on a Mexican table as it would be in England or France. It is a special ingredient, or the careful choice of a combination of unusual ingredients, that turns roast pork into a Mexican dish, for example, by adding a chilli-based seasoning and a little orange juice to the gravy.

Pork plays a leading role in the Mexican kitchen, perhaps because the Aztecs used to cook wild pigs before the Conquest. Or it could be that pigs are easier to rear on maize cobs and other natural waste foods from the kitchen. Lamb is popular mostly as *barbacoa* (see page 147), while goat is mostly enjoyed roasted over an open fire. In Mexico beef is considerably more expensive and is often very tough, hence the need to boil it for hours to soften it, leaving a nutritious stock to turn into a *sopa aguada* (watery soup).

Roasting is not a well known way of cooking meat in Mexico; it is generally grilled or boiled, and then shredded. Cuts of meat are lean and fat is not included on the joints, though it is added in the frying. The cuts are very different from those found in England; Mexican butchers take great pride in removing every bit of gristle and sinew that could spoil the meat, and they also seem to cut around the natural grain of the meat rather than across it. The custom of shredding meat or serving it in small pieces probably comes from their use as a filling for *tacos*, for which carving is not necessary.

Albondigas al Chilpotle

MEATBALLS IN SMOKED *JALAPEÑO* SAUCE

SERVES 4

Meatballs are extremely popular in Mexico. They are usually eaten in a spicy tomato or chilli sauce, accompanied by rice and green vegetables, such as *chayotes* and *calabacitas*, and soft warm *tortillas*.

INGREDIENTS

225 g (8 oz) finely minced beef	1/4 teaspoon ground black pepper
225 g (8 oz) finely minced pork	pinch of sugar
1 slice of bread, soaked in water, then drained	oil
1 tablespoon malt vinegar	1 quantity hot *Salsa de Chile Chilpotle* (see page 38) or any other type of salsa
1/2 teaspoon salt	

METHOD

■ Mix the meats, bread, vinegar, salt, pepper and sugar together and leave for 1 hour. Drain off any juices, then shape the mixture into chestnut-sized meatballs.

■ Heat some oil in a frying pan, add the meatballs, cover and fry over low heat for 5 minutes. Uncover and turn the meatballs, then continue frying until brown all over. Remove and drain on absorbent kitchen paper. Place the meatballs in a heated ovenproof casserole, pour over the hot sauce, cover and cook in the oven at 170°C, 325°F, Gas Mark 3 for 20 minutes. Serve hot.

VARIATIONS

ALBONDIGUITAS (**Baby Meatballs**) Make the meatballs even smaller and serve on cocktail sticks with the *salsa* in a dish to dip them in. Serve as canapés.

Frijoles al Arriero

———— TIPSY BEANS ————

ᐱᐯᐱ

SERVES 6

For a hearty supper, this is a good meal in one, or it can be served as a side dish for a buffet dinner. It goes well with a green salad and soft warm *tortillas*.

INGREDIENTS

225 g (8 oz) dried beans (any type)	100 g (4 oz) bacon, chopped
1 knuckle of pork	100 g (4 oz) chorizo, sliced
225 g (8 oz) boned shoulder of pork in 1 piece	1/2 onion, finely chopped
	2 green chillies
1 clove garlic	4 tomatoes, chopped
1 teaspoon salt	350 ml (12 fl oz) beer
1 teaspoon sugar	4 tablespoons chopped fresh coriander
2 tablespoons oil	fresh coriander, to garnish

METHOD

■ Remove any small stones and debris from the beans, place them in a sieve and wash them under running water until the water runs clear. Place them in a large saucepan, and cover with cold water, adding enough water to come 10 cm (5 inches) above the surface of the beans. Leave to soak overnight. (If you have forgotten to soak the beans overnight, clean and rinse them, then cook them in rapidly boiling water for 15 minutes. Cover the pan with a tight-fitting lid and remove from the heat. Leave to stand for 1 hour.)

■ Add the meat and garlic to the beans, cover and simmer for up to 3 hours or until the meat and beans are tender, adding more boiling water if required. Add the salt and sugar, and simmer for a further 10 minutes.

■ Remove any meat from the knuckle and discard the bone and skin. Return any meat to the pan. Cut the pork shoulder into bite-sized pieces and return to the pan. In a separate frying pan, heat the oil and fry the bacon and *chorizo* until crisp, then add all the remaining ingredients, except the beer and coriander. Continue to fry for 5 minutes, then add to the beans with the beer and coriander. Simmer, uncovered, until the beans have absorbed the extra liquid. The finished dish should not be too dry; it should have some sauce. Garnish with fresh coriander.

Carne Frita

CRISPY FRIED SHREDDED MEAT

SERVES 4

*C*arne frita is the term used for any type of meat or chicken which has been boiled or roasted, then shredded and fried with chopped onions until crisp. The meat is used as a filling for *burritos* or soft warm wheat or corn *tortillas*, accompanied by a *salsa* and *guacamole*, and garnished with lettuce. It is a good way of using up leftover meat.

INGREDIENTS

2 tablespoons oil	1 green chilli, finely sliced
¹/₂ onion, finely chopped	¹/₂ teaspoon salt
450 g (1 lb) cooked meat, finely shredded	¹/₄ teaspoon ground black pepper

METHOD

■ Heat the oil and fry the onion for about 4 minutes or until golden. Add the meat, chilli, salt and pepper, and fry for 15 minutes, tossing, until the meat becomes dry and very crisp. Serve hot.

Chile con Carne

BEEF IN A SPICY CHILLI BEAN SAUCE

SERVES 10–12

*C*hile con Carne is almost unknown in Mexico. It is a very good Tex-Mex dish which I imagine started as an American interpretation of our traditional Mexican dish, *Molli* (see page 122), which is served with beans and rice. However, because everyone outside Mexico expects to find a recipe for *Chile con Carne* in a Mexican cookery book, I have included my Mexican version.

This recipe is good for a main course for a party of 10–12 people, but you could halve or quarter the amounts for smaller numbers; it is also a good filling for *Burritos Norteños*. Serve with any of the rice recipes and a mixed salad.

INGREDIENTS

1 kg (2 lb) stewing steak, cubed or minced	¹/₂ teaspoon dried marjoram
2 tablespoons malt vinegar	¹/₂ teaspoon dried thyme
³/₄ teaspoon salt	¹/₂ teaspoon ground cinnamon
¹/₂ teaspoon ground black pepper	12 cloves
¹/₄ teaspoon sugar	¹/₂ teaspoon cumin seeds
6 tablespoons oil	¹/₂ teaspoon aniseed
2 bay leaves	1 tablespoon cayenne pepper
750 ml (1¹/₄ pints) water	1 teaspoon sesame seeds
2 cloves garlic	750 g (1¹/₂ lb) canned peeled tomatoes, mashed
1 large onion	
4 tablespoons *mole* powder or 2 tablespoons chilli powder	6 tablespoons tomato purée
6 sprigs fresh coriander	1 quantity cooked *Frijoles* and their liquid (see page 28)
¹/₂ teaspoon dried oregano	

METHOD

■ Season the meat with the vinegar, salt, pepper and sugar. Cover and leave to marinate overnight in the refrigerator.

■ Heat the oil in a large flameproof casserole and fry the meat until golden brown. Drain off excess oil and reserve it. Add the bay leaves and water to the meat, cover and simmer for about 1 hour or until tender. Drain and reserve the stock, and discard the bay leaves. Put 150 ml (¹/₄ pint) of the stock in a blender, and add the garlic, onion, *mole* or chilli powder, herbs, spices and sesame seeds. Blend to a smooth paste.

■ Heat the reserved oil in a frying pan, and fry the paste for about 4 minutes, stirring continually, until it dries a little. Add the mashed tomatoes, tomato purée and remaining stock. Simmer for 20 minutes, then add the cooked beans and their liquid, and simmer for 15 minutes. Add the meat and continue simmering very gently for 30 minutes, stirring frequently. Serve hot.

Cecina

MEXICAN CURED BEEF

MAKES about
450 g (1 lb)

Cecina is usually beef, cured and dried in very thin slices, although pork or venison are often used. This is very definitely a food from the north of Mexico where there is abundant cattle and distances are great. Travellers in days gone by had to traverse mountains, valleys and deserts and carry as little as possible, so *cecina* was a must.

Cecina is used very much like *chorizo*; it can be mixed with scrambled eggs or cooked in a sauce for filling *tacos* and *burritos*. In England it is possible to ask your butcher to cut a joint of silverside along the grain, as thinly as he possibly can and in such a way that as he approaches the end of the piece he is cutting from, he does not cut through but turns the piece round and starts cutting from the other end, giving a concertina effect and thus avoiding having many little pieces of meat in favour of one long strand.

For the best and most authentic results, this meat should be dried in strong sunshine! If this is impossible, cut it as instructed, marinate it and keep it in the refrigerator for 1–2 days.

INGREDIENTS

750 g (1½ lb) silverside, very thinly sliced	½ teaspoon dried mixed herbs
1½ teaspoons salt	1 teaspoon dried chilli powder
4 tablespoons malt vinegar	

METHOD

■ Once the meat has been cut, mix together the salt, vinegar, herbs and chilli powder, and rub over both sides of the meat. Fold it back to its original 'one piece' and leave in a cool place for 2 hours. (The juices of the meat will start dripping out so when you hang it up to dry, remember to use a tray to catch them.)

■ Hang the meat for 1 day in the sunshine (away from birds, cats and dogs) until it is dry but not stiff. Move the meat to a cool, dry place and hang again to 'air'. When aired and quite dry, pound it with a meat hammer and keep refrigerated. The meat will continue drying in the fridge, so you may cover it with a well oiled piece of greaseproof paper. The *cecina* is now ready to use.

Guisado de Cecina para Burritos o Tacos

—— STEWED *CECINA* TO FILL *BURRITOS, TACOS* OR *FAJITAS* ——

SERVES 4

The flavour of *cecina* is well concentrated when it has been dried; it makes a tasty filling when combined with onion, garlic, chillies and tomatoes.

INGREDIENTS

1 quantity *Cecina* (see page 134)	2 green chillies
2 onions, charred (see page 43)	pinch of salt (if needed)
2 garlic cloves, charred (see page 43)	4 tablespoons oil
6 tomatoes, charred and peeled (see page 43)	100 ml (4 fl oz) water

METHOD

■ Lightly oil a griddle or heavy-based frying pan, heat it, and cook the *cecina* on it until it looks quite dry but not burnt. Remove the *cecina* from the heat, let it cool, and then break it into small pieces, shredding it as you go along.

■ Put the onions, garlic, tomatoes, chillies and salt in a food processor, and blend to a purée. Heat the oil in a frying pan, add the purée and meat, and fry, stirring until dry. Add the water and simmer until the sauce thickens. Use to fill *burritos*, corn *tortilla tacos* or *fajitas* with a little *guacamole*.

Carne Deshebrada

—— SHREDDED BEEF SALAD ——

SERVES 4

*C*arne Deshebrada or *Ropa Vieja* is used as a main course, often served with rice and soft, warm corn *tortillas* for each person to make *tacos* with. It is a popular way of eating tough meat which is boiled until soft. The meat traditionally used is beef skirt, but stewing steak is also very good. To make shredding easier, the meat must be cooked until it is almost falling apart.

INGREDIENTS

450 g (1 lb) beef skirt	2 tablespoons finely chopped fresh coriander
1 litre (1³/₄ pints) water	2 green chillies, finely chopped
1 large onion, charred and halved (see page 43)	juice of 1 lime or lemon
1 clove garlic, charred (see page 43)	¹/₂ teaspoon salt
1 bay leaf	¹/₂ teaspoon ground black pepper
1 tablespoon vinegar	¹/₂ lettuce, finely shredded
2 tomatoes, finely chopped	2 ripe avocados and 8 radishes, sliced, to garnish
¹/₂ onion, finely chopped	

METHOD

■ Put the beef in a saucepan with the water, halved onion, garlic, bay leaf and vinegar. Cover and boil for at least 1¹/₂ hours or until the meat is very tender and falls apart. Leave the meat to cool in the stock.

■ Remove the meat from the stock (use the stock for soup). Shred the meat finely and mix with the tomatoes, chopped onion, coriander and chillies. Mix the lime or lemon juice with the salt and pepper, and pour it over the meat. Mix well. Arrange the lettuce around the edge of a serving dish, and place the meat in the centre. Just before serving, halve, stone, peel and slice the avocados and use as garnish with the radish slices.

Hígados Encebollados

FRIED LIVER AND ONIONS

SERVES 4

I am not very fond of liver, which is why I find this recipe so appealing – it actually makes liver taste good. It is best eaten with rice of any type and green vegetables. In Mexico, ox liver is normally used and the butcher peels off the membrane which would cause the liver to shrink when fried and make it difficult to chew. Cut the cooking time by half if you prefer to use lamb's or calf's liver. Cut into long strips after cooking and mixed with the onions, the liver makes a delicious filling for *tacos* or *fajitas*.

INGREDIENTS

450 g (1 lb) liver, thinly sliced	1 clove garlic, crushed
1 tablespoon malt vinegar	2 green chillies, finely chopped
1/2 teaspoon salt	3 tablespoons oil
1/4 teaspoon ground black pepper	1 large onion, finely sliced

METHOD

■ Season the liver with the vinegar, salt, pepper, garlic and chillies, and leave to marinate for 20 minutes. Heat the oil in a heavy-based frying pan and fry the liver over moderate heat for 4 minutes. Turn and fry the other side for 4 minutes. Transfer to a heated serving dish and keep warm. Add the onion to the pan, sprinkle with salt and pepper, and fry for about 3 minutes, stirring frequently. Garnish the liver with the onion and serve immediately.

Pancita

———————— TRIPE IN TOMATO SAUCE AND SPICES ————————

SERVES 4

Tripe is a very popular dish in the north of Mexico. It is also used for soup as in *Menudo* (see page 87) and very much enjoyed. In England it is always sold very clean and fresh, and it makes a hearty dish. The sauce is delicious with rice or mashed potato to soak it up. Begin preparations the day before.

INGREDIENTS

1 lemon	1 onion, finely chopped
1 kg (2 lb) tripe	3 tablespoons tomato purée
2 bay leaves	$1/2$ teaspoon salt
4 cloves	8 whole peppercorns
600 ml (1 pint) water	3 green chillies
2 tablespoons oil	4 tablespoons chopped fresh parsley

METHOD

■ Peel the rind from the lemon and reserve. Cut the lemon in half. Wash the tripe and pat dry with absorbent kitchen paper, then clean it by rubbing it all over with the lemon, squeezing some of the lemon juice as you go along. Put the tripe in a saucepan with the lemon rind, bay leaves, cloves and water. Cover and simmer for $2^{1}/_{2}$ hours or until very tender (the meat should be falling apart). Strain off the liquid, allow to cool, then refrigerate. Carefully cut the tripe into serving portions, cover, and refrigerate overnight.

■ The next day, discard any grease from the surface of the stock. Heat the oil in a saucepan, and sauté the onion until soft. Add the tomato purée, salt, peppercorns, chillies, parsley and stock. Simmer, uncovered, for 15 minutes or until the liquid is reduced by one third. Add the tripe, reheat gently and serve hot. Remove and discard the chillies, if preferred, or chop them and return them to the dish.

Picadillo

MINCED MEAT WITH OLIVES AND RAISINS IN TOMATO SAUCE

SERVES 4;
fills 6 individual
empanadas or
6 *Chiles Rellenos*

*P*icadillo is the most popular way of cooking minced meat in Mexico and, to my mind, the most tasty. It is often used as a filling for *Chiles Rellenos* and *empanadas* or *tacos*, but it is also served with rice and *Rajas de Chile Poblano* (see page 170) for a nice supper or light lunch.

INGREDIENTS

100 g (4 oz) finely minced beef	1 red pepper, deseeded and sliced
100 g (4 oz) finely minced pork	3 sticks celery, finely chopped
2 teaspoons malt vinegar	1 chicken stock cube, crumbled
1/4 teaspoon salt	1 small potato, cooked and cubed
1/4 teaspoon ground black pepper	9 stuffed green olives, sliced
1/4 teaspoon sugar	2 teaspoons flaked almonds
1 tablespoon oil	2 tablespoons raisins
1/2 onion, finely chopped	450 g (1 lb) canned tomatoes
1 clove garlic, crushed	2 tablespoons tomato purée
1 green chilli, chopped	

METHOD

■ Mix the minced meats together and season with the vinegar, salt, pepper and sugar. Heat the oil in a large frying pan, and fry the onion, garlic, chilli, red pepper and celery for 3 minutes. Add the meat and stir over high heat for about 10 minutes or until it starts to brown. (This can sometimes take longer than you would expect if the vegetables have a high water content, so just continue frying until the liquid is absorbed).

■ Drain off any surplus oil, taking care to retain the meat juices, and add the remaining ingredients. Simmer for 15 minutes or until the mixture starts to dry out, stirring occasionally. Serve hot or, if using as a filling, allow to cool.

Tacos al Carbon

BEEF *TACOS*

SERVES 6

In Mexico City, *taquerías* (shops selling nothing but *tacos*), are numerous, and the range of different varieties of *taco* they sell is remarkable. Virtually every kind of meat and vegetable, and every imaginable combination of sauces, are used, as well as melted cheese. The *tacos* in this recipe are particularly good for an outdoor barbecue. The meat I use is beef skirt, which is available if you order it in advance, but it is important to marinate it and to slice it against the grain very thinly, otherwise it could be quite tough. Serve inside soft warm corn *tortillas* with either *Guacamole*, *Salsa Típica* or *Salsa de Tomate Verde* and/or soured cream as well as *Jalapeños en Vinagre*. Preparation starts the day before.

INGREDIENTS

1 kg (2 lb) beef skirt (flank)	¼ teaspoon sugar
MARINADE	2 cloves garlic, charred and crushed (see page 43)
2 tablespoons olive oil	
2 tablespoons malt vinegar	½ teaspoon salt
1 tablespoon lemon juice	½ onion, sliced
½ teaspoon dried oregano	¼ teaspoon ground black pepper

METHOD

■ Mix together all the ingredients for the marinade. Put the meat in a non-metallic container and spoon the marinade over it, making sure all the meat is coated. Cover and leave to marinate in the refrigerator overnight, or longer if possible.

■ Remove the meat from the marinade and cook on the barbecue for 15–20 minutes. Carve the meat into thin strips, cutting on a slant against the grain. Place strips of meat in the middle of soft warm corn *tortillas*, bathe with sauce, soured cream and pickles, roll up and eat immediately.

Carnitas

MARINATED ROAST PORK

SERVES 4

This traditional dish from Michoacán is now prepared in most Mexican restaurants because of its popularity. It is another example of the Mexican's love for soft *tacos*. Whether you buy the *Carnitas* ready-made to take home, eat them in a restaurant or prepare them yourself, you will enjoy one of the best ways of eating pork you have ever tried.

Carnitas must always be fried in pork fat. It is impressive to see the *peroles*, enormous copper pots big enough to have a bath in, sitting on top of wood fires, bubbling with the hot fat to which the meat has been added. To avoid sticking, the cooks use large wooden paddles which look like oars. This, of course, produces the very top quality *Carnitas* with the best flavour; I sincerely hope that this procedure never changes. However, in Britain we have to improvise and use the equipment at hand while trying to preserve authenticity. Preparation starts the night before.

INGREDIENTS

1 onion, charred (see page 43)	¹/₄ teaspoon sugar
3 cloves garlic, charred (see page 43)	300 ml (¹/₂ pint) evaporated milk
3 tablespoons malt vinegar	1.5 kg (3 lb) shoulder of pork, skin removed
¹/₂ teaspoon salt	
¹/₂ teaspoon ground black pepper	300 ml (¹/₂ pint) water
1 teaspoon mixed dried herbs	1.5 kg (3 lb) pork fat

METHOD

■ Put the onion, garlic, vinegar, salt, black pepper, herbs, sugar and milk in a blender and purée to a paste. Rub the paste well over the meat, then cover and leave to marinate overnight in the refrigerator.

■ Put the meat and marinade in a deep ovenproof dish, and pour over the water. Add the pork fat and bake in a preheated oven at 170°C, 325°F, Gas Mark 3 for about 2 hours, basting and turning occasionally, until the meat is tender and falling off the bone. Drain off all the fat. At the bottom of the dish you will find the meat gravy. Serve the meat off the bone, pour the gravy over it and use as a filling for warm *tortillas*, accompanied by *guacamole* and any of the *salsas*.

Chorizo Picante

———— SPICY PORK SAUSAGE WITH *ANCHO* CHILLIES ————

MAKES 450 g
(1 lb)

Small amounts of *chorizo* are used as a flavouring in many Mexican dishes. It's flavour is strong and *chorizo* is usually only eaten by itself sliced very thinly on bread and butter, similar to the way the French eat *saucisson*. Commercial *chorizo* is now available from some large supermarket delicatessens. This recipe calls for *ancho* chillies which are now available in England from speciality shops, but if you cannot find any, use chilli powder instead.

INGREDIENTS

8 *ancho* chillies or 2 tablespoons chilli powder

300 ml ($^1\!/_2$ pint) boiling water

2 cloves garlic, crushed

1 tablespoon tomato purée

$^1\!/_2$ teaspoon dried oregano

$^1\!/_2$ teaspoon salt

$^1\!/_4$ teaspoon cumin

$^1\!/_4$ teaspoon cayenne pepper

$^1\!/_4$ teaspoon ground black pepper

$^1\!/_4$ teaspoon sugar

75 ml (3 fl oz) vinegar

450 g (1 lb) shoulder of pork, finely minced

METHOD

■ Heat the chillies in a dry frying pan for about 3 minutes or until soft, turning frequently. Discard the stems and seeds, and put the chillies in a bowl. Cover with the boiling water and leave to soak for 1 hour. Drain, then work to a paste in a blender or food processor with all the remaining ingredients, except the pork. Mix the paste thoroughly into the meat. Store in the fridge for 4 days in an uncovered non-metallic container, stirring and draining off any liquid twice daily. The *chorizo* will keep, refrigerated, for about 2 weeks, if stirred daily. Fry in hot oil until crisp and serve with beans, rice or eggs or as a garnish for *antojitos*.

Costillitas Adobadas

SPARE RIBS IN CHILLI AND CREAM SAUCE

SERVES 4

Ideal for an outdoor barbecue party, spare ribs are very tasty with *ancho* chilli sauce spread on them. You need to use the long-boned spare ribs. Serve with beans, rice, salad, warm *tortillas*, *Elote Asados* and *Cebollitas Asadas* (see pages 163 and 158). Preparation should start 2 hours in advance.

INGREDIENTS

3 *ancho* chillies	¹/₄ onion, finely chopped
150 ml (¹/₄ pint) single cream	1.5 kg (3 lb) pork spare ribs
2 tomatoes, grilled and skinned	3 tablespoons malt vinegar
¹/₂ teaspoon sugar	2¹/₂ teaspoons salt
1 clove garlic, crushed	¹/₄ teaspoon ground black pepper
1 chicken stock cube	

METHOD

■ Wash the chillies in very hot water to soften them. Remove the stalks and seeds, and soak the chillies in the cream for at least 2 hours.

■ Put the chillies and the cream in a blender with the tomatoes, sugar, garlic, chicken stock cube and onion, and blend to a paste. Rub through a sieve and set aside. Trim off any excess fat from the spare ribs. Sprinkle the ribs with the vinegar, salt and pepper, and marinate for 2 hours.

■ When the barbecue flames start to die down, grill the ribs for about 10 minutes on each side, turning them so they cook evenly. Brush them liberally with the chilli sauce and continue cooking on all sides for 4–5 minutes more. Serve hot.

VARIATION

You can make this dish indoors by roasting the unseasoned spare ribs in the oven at 180°C, 350°F, Gas Mark 4 for 30 minutes. Drain off any excess fat from the pan, season the ribs, pour over the sauce and continue baking for another 30 minutes, basting frequently.

Cochinita Pibil

STEAMED PORK

▲▼▲

SERVES 4

Cochinita Pibil is popular throughout Mexico but it originated in Yucatán. It takes its name from the traditional way of cooking it in a *pib*, which is Mayan for 'hole in the ground'. As for *barbacoa*, a hole is dug in the ground and filled with red-hot stones, followed by the meat, seasoned and wrapped in banana leaves. Fortunately, however, the dish can also be prepared in your own oven, simply by wrapping the meat in well greased waxed paper, inside a square of kitchen foil. Preparation starts the day before so that you can marinate the pork.

Achiote, a paste made from annatto seeds, diluted with Seville orange or grapefruit juice, is used as a seasoning in this dish. It is red in colour, but not at all hot, and makes meats and fish very tasty, tenderizing them by marinating and steaming. In England, Indian shops sell *tandoori* mixture, which is similar to *achiote* and therefore makes a good substitute.

INGREDIENTS

1 kg (2 lb) hand of pork	juice of 2 Seville oranges or 1 grapefruit
1 large purple onion, sliced into rings	2 cloves garlic, crushed
MARINADE	¹/₂ teaspoon dried oregano
¹/₂ teaspoon salt	¹/₂ teaspoon ground cumin
¹/₂ teaspoon ground black pepper	4 tablespoons *achiote* or *tandoori* mixture
pinch of sugar	

METHOD

■ Mix all the marinade ingredients together to a smooth paste and rub it generously over the meat. Cover and refrigerate for 24 hours.

■ Wrap the meat in well greased waxed paper and overwrap in kitchen foil. Place the meat in a baking dish, cover and bake in the oven at 170°C, 325°F, Gas Mark 3 for 3¹/₂ hours or until the meat is extremely tender and falling off the bone. Unwrap just before serving, arrange on a warm dish and garnish with onion rings. Serve hot with warm *tortillas*, rice, beans and salad.

OPPOSITE *Chiles Rellenos de Queso* (peppers stuffed with cheese, coated and fried in egg batter, served with hot tomato sauce, page 160). The photograph shows three stages of the dish: in the red bowl is a scorched pepper ready for peeling; the frying pan contains two peeled, stuffed peppers that have been secured with cocktail sticks and dipped in egg batter, and are being fried in hot oil; the peppers are then oven baked in tomato sauce and garnished with grated cheese. The oval dish shows the finished recipe.

Cazuela Tabasqueña

MEAT, BEANS AND PLANTAIN CASSEROLE

∧∨∧

SERVES 8

This casserole is traditionally made with shredded beef or pork and black beans but any other type of beans can be used as long as they are first cooked as instructed on page 28. The dish originates from a very tropical part of Mexico where plantains grow in abundance.

INGREDIENTS

2 very ripe plantains	1 tablespoon malt vinegar
600 ml (1 pint) water	$^1/_2$ teaspoon salt
100 g (4 oz) butter	$^1/_4$ teaspoon ground allspice
450 g (1 lb) beef skirt or pork shoulder, cubed	TO FINISH
	1 tablespoon oil
2 sticks celery	1 onion, finely chopped
2 cabbage leaves	2 green chillies, finely chopped
1 carrot	2 tablespoons tomato purée
1 clove garlic	1 beef stock cube
1 bay leaf	$^1/_2$ quantity *Frijoles Refritos* (see page 31)

METHOD

■ Quarter the plantains, leaving the skins on, and boil them in the water for 15 minutes or until soft. Drain, reserving the water. Peel the plantains and remove the centre veins, then mash them to a pulp with half the butter.

■ Boil the meat in the reserved water with the vegetables, garlic, bay leaf, vinegar, salt and allspice, for about 40 minutes until tender. Drain, reserving the liquid. Shred the meat finely.

■ Heat the oil in a frying pan and fry the onion and chillies for 5 minutes. Add the shredded meat and fry for 5 minutes, stirring occasionally. Add the tomato purée, reserved liquid and beef stock cube and simmer, uncovered, for 15 minutes or until the sauce thickens.

■ Grease an ovenproof dish liberally, put the beans in the bottom, then cover with the meat and sauce. Finally, add the plantain purée. Dot with the remaining butter and bake in the oven at 180°C, 350°F, Gas Mark 4 for 30 minutes.

OPPOSITE   Clockwise from top: *Costillitas Adobadas* (spare ribs in chilli and cream sauce, page 143), *Cebollitas Asadas* (grilled spring onions, page 158) and *Elotes Asados* (roast corn on the cob, page 163)

Patitas de Puerco a la Mexicana

PIG'S TROTTERS IN TOMATO SAUCE

SERVES 4

The first time I served a Mexican buffet dinner at our home, about fifteen years ago, at the request of friends we had invited, I decided to include this as a side dish. My husband disapproved. 'You cannot serve pig's trotters for dinner to guests! You will not serve these at our home!' he said. But I am stubborn by nature, and even more stubborn when I know I am right, so I went ahead and prepared the dish and smuggled it on to the table amongst all the others. During the meal my husband passed the small dish to one of our guests, saying, 'Try this. I am not sure what it is but it is delicious!' Eventually he asked, in a loud voice, 'Lourdes, what is this dish?' 'Pig's trotters,' I replied. We all had a good laugh as someone claimed the last bit of sauce. Rice, boiled carrots and mashed potatoes go extremely well with this dish. Preparation starts the day before.

INGREDIENTS

2 lemons	1 onion, finely chopped
3 pig's trotters	3 tablespoons tomato purée
225 g (8 oz) stewing pork, cubed	$^1/_2$ teaspoon salt
2 bay leaves	8 peppercorns
4 cloves	3 green chillies
600 ml (1 pint) water	4 tablespoons chopped fresh parsley
2 tablespoons oil	

METHOD

■ Peel the rind from the lemons and reserve. Cut the lemons in half. Wash the pig's trotters and pat dry with absorbent kitchen paper, then clean them by rubbing all over with the lemon halves, squeezing out some of the juice as you go. Put the trotters in a large saucepan with the pork, lemon rind, bay leaves, cloves and water. Cover and bring to the boil, then simmer for $2^1/_2$ hours or until the meat is very tender and falling off the bone. Strain off the liquid, and pick out all the bones. Return the meat to the stock, cool and refrigerate overnight.

■ Carefully remove and discard the fat from the top of the stock. Heat the oil in a large saucepan, and sauté the onion until soft. Add the tomato purée, salt, peppercorns, chillies, parsley and stock, and simmer, uncovered, for 15 minutes or until reduced by one third. Add the trotters and the meat. Reheat gently and serve hot.

Barbacoa

LAMB IN BEER MARINADE

∿∿∿

SERVES 4

Barbacoa means 'from chin to tail', and refers to the original method of cooking a lamb in a hole in the ground on top of red-hot stones. This is probably the origin of the word 'barbecue'. In Mexico, it is almost always lamb that is chosen for this style of cooking. The animal is cleaned and seasoned with salt and spices, wrapped in *agave* leaves, and then steamed for about 15 hours. The extremely slow cooking and the *agave* help give the meat a delicious flavour. As I do not imagine you wish to dig up your garden, I have adapted the traditional recipe so that it is suitable for cooking smaller pieces of lamb in a conventional oven. Preparation begins the night before.

Barbacoa is ideal for a buffet, accompanied by other *taco* fillings, such as *Guacamole, Salsa Borracha, Arroz Blanco, Frijoles, Salpicón de Hongos* and *Quesadillas*, a tossed salad and masses of warm *tortillas*. Let everyone help themselves and make up their own *tacos* in a sort of finger-food fashion.

INGREDIENTS

1 kg (2 lb) shoulder of lamb	1 bay leaf
2 tablespoons malt vinegar	1 large onion, quartered
¹/₂ teaspoon salt	pinch of dried oregano
¹/₄ teaspoon ground black pepper	2 green chillies
¹/₄ teaspoon sugar	TO SERVE
two 350 ml (12 fl oz) cans of Mexican beer or lager	bunch of radishes, sliced
4 cloves garlic , crushed	¹/₂ onion, finely sliced
	warm corn *tortillas* (see page 24)

METHOD

■ Place the meat in a non-metallic dish and season it with the vinegar, salt, pepper and sugar. Pour in the beer and add the garlic, bay leaf, onion, oregano and chillies. Cover and leave for 8 hours or overnight. Turn twice.

■ Put the marinade in a baking tin, place the meat on a rack above, and roast in the oven at 170°C, 325°F, Gas Mark 3 for 3 hours, basting frequently, until the meat is very tender and falls away from the bone. Cut the meat into bite-sized pieces. Place on a serving dish and keep warm.

■ Boil the pan juices for 10 minutes or until reduced by half. Strain and, with the back of a spoon, push the cooked onion and garlic through the sieve to thicken the sauce. Adjust the seasoning and pour over the meat. Serve hot, garnished with sliced radishes and onions, and accompanied by warm *tortillas*. To make *tacos*, put some meat, your choice of sauce, radishes, *guacamole*, and onion along the centre of a warm *tortilla*, then roll up and eat.

Birria

MARINATED LAMB WITH *CHILE ANCHO*

SERVES 8

This dish is so popular in Guadalajara that there are restaurants that specialise in it called *birrierías*. The choice of meat varies as it can be a combination of pork, veal and lamb or mutton or any meat on its own. The consistency of the dish also varies from a liquid soup to a thicker stew, the latter being my favourite because it can be used as a filling for corn or flour *tortillas* to make soft *tacos* or the popular *fajitas*. The marinade can be made with *chiles anchos* or any variety of available dried chillies. The cook is the creator of this dish and so long as the result is tasty, you can vary it as you please. Begin preparations the day before.

INGREDIENTS

ancho chillies	1¹/₂ onions, charred and quartered (see page 43)
600 ml (1 pint) boiling water	1 teaspoon dried oregano
4 tablespoons malt or wine vinegar	¹/₂ teaspoon ground cumin
2 kg (4 lb) shoulder of lamb	600 ml (1 pint) plus 4 tablespoons cold water
³/₄ teaspoon salt	
¹/₂ teaspoon ground black pepper	1 tablespoon cornflour
¹/₄ teaspoon sugar	¹/₂ onion, finely chopped
4 cloves garlic, charred (see page 43)	

METHOD

■ Roast the chillies on a hot griddle or in a heavy-based frying pan, turning them frequently until they become soft and pliable. Remove the stalks, seeds and veins, and soak the chillies in the boiling water for about 1 hour. Meanwhile, pour the vinegar over the lamb and sprinkle with salt, pepper and sugar. When the chillies become soft, place them with their liquid in a blender, together with the garlic, onions, oregano and cumin, and blend to a paste. Rub the paste over the lamb, cover and leave to marinate overnight in the refrigerator.

■ Place the lamb on a rack in a roasting tin. Pour the 600 ml (1 pint) cold water into the roasting tin and cover with two layers of kitchen foil. Roast in the oven at 170°C, 325°F, Gas Mark 3 for 3–4 hours or until the meat is falling off the bone, basting frequently. Remove the meat and keep warm. Mix the cornflour with the 4 tablespoons cold water and add to the juices left in the roasting tin, stirring all the time. Simmer until the gravy thickens. Traditionally this meat is not sliced for serving, but is separated into long strands which are then placed on warm corn or flour *tortillas*, garnished with raw chopped onion and served with a little of the meat gravy.

Mixiotes

STEAMED LAMB PARCELS

SERVES 6

Mixiotes can be made with any meat, but lamb seems to be the favourite. Traditionally, they are steamed in the skin peeled off the *agave* leaf and tied into bundles that resemble money purses. *Nopalitos* (cactus paddles) are often cooked together with the meat, but they are not essential. As the *agave* is unobtainable outside Mexico, I make the parcels from squares of grease-proof paper and kitchen foil. Since the dish needs to be marinated, start the day before.

INGREDIENTS

1.5 kg (3 lb) shoulder of lamb, cubed	¼ teaspoon dried thyme
½ teaspoon salt	¼ teaspoon ground cumin
½ teaspoon ground black pepper	¼ teaspoon dried marjoram
3 tablespoons malt vinegar	pinch of ground allspice
6 *chiles guajillos* or chilli powder	2 sprigs fresh *epazote* or basil
4 *chiles pasilla* or paprika	3 cloves garlic, charred (see page 43)
½ teaspoon dried oregano	3 bottles of Mexican beer or lager

METHOD

■ Season the meat with the salt, pepper and vinegar. Heat the dried chillies on a hot griddle or heavy-based frying pan until soft. Discard the seeds, veins and stems, and put the chillies in a blender with all the herbs and spices, the garlic and 1 bottle beer. Leave to soak for 20 minutes, then blend to a purée. Cover the meat with the purée and leave to marinate overnight in the refrigerator.

■ Cut twelve 20 cm (8 inch) squares of greaseproof paper, and twelve 20 cm (8 inch) squares of kitchen foil. Place a square of paper over a square of foil and spoon a little meat and some juice in the centre. Pull the four sides together, and tie securely, ensuring there are no holes for the juices to escape. Repeat until all the parcels are tied. Place the parcels carefully in the top of a steamer that has the remainder of the beer in its base. Steam the *Mixiotes* for 2–2½ hours. It is important to put a few small stones in the bottom of the steamer. When the beer evaporates, the stones will start jumping and alert you to add more water. Serve hot with refried beans and warm *tortillas*.

VEGETABLES AND SALADS

▲▲▲▲▲▲▲▲▲▲▲▲▲▲▲▲▲

THIS chapter has been written with vegetarians in mind. It seems that in Mexico no vegetable is served just as it is; we always cook it with a little of this and a little of that! The results are not only ingenious, but also tasty and nutritious.

Mexico is a vegetarian's paradise, as practically any fruit or vegetable can be grown in the country at any time of the year. If you look hard enough, you can always find what you are after, even if it is out of season.

Dried beans feature prominently in Mexican cookery, often used refried by themselves, for *antojitos*, or soups. Eaten three times a day, they are an important staple in the Mexican diet.

Salads, too, play an important part in the Mexican kitchen. If they contain meat, chicken or fish, they are mostly used as light meals or fillings for warm, soft *tortillas*. Lettuce is used to garnish many *antojitos* and as a garnish for almost any type of hot food. Any salad you wish to prepare will enhance a Mexican meal, especially if you combine lemon or lime juice instead of vinegar with olive oil to make the dressing. Sliced tomatoes and finely sliced onions, as well as radishes cut in the shape of flowers, add a very Mexican touch, as do fresh coriander, very finely shredded lettuce and avocado slices. In this chapter, I have concentrated on vegetable salads; meat, fish or chicken salads can be found in other chapters.

Budin de Flor de Calabaza

TORTILLA AND CHEESE CASSEROLE WITH COURGETTE BLOSSOMS

᭛᭛᭛

SERVES 4

I love eating flowers, and courgette and marrow blossoms are so attractive and appetising that they can also be used to garnish the dish. This casserole is similar to *Budin Azteca* but includes courgette blossoms and egg instead of chicken, so you can surprise your vegetarian friends with yet another unusual dish. It is suitable as a buffet or luncheon dish accompanied by *Frijoles Refritos* and a tossed salad. You can use bought ready-salted *tortilla* chips instead of frying your own *tortillas*. Courgette flowers can occasionally be found in Italian shops as the Italians eat them too. Otherwise, I collect them from my own plants as soon as they pollinate, and freeze them until I have enough to make a dish.

INGREDIENTS

oil	¼ teaspoon salt
8 corn *tortillas* (see page 24)	¼ teaspoon ground black pepper
25 g (1 oz) butter	75 ml (3 fl oz) single cream
½ onion, chopped	150 ml (¼ pint) soured cream
1 green chilli, finely chopped	5 tablespoons grated Cheddar cheese
4 *epazote* or coriander leaves, finely chopped	75 g (3 oz) mozzarella cheese, grated
2 tomatoes, grilled, peeled and crushed	2 eggs, well beaten
450 g (1 lb) courgette blossoms or 275 g (10 oz) cooked spinach, chopped	courgette blossoms or sprigs of fresh parsley, to garnish

METHOD

■ Heat some oil in a frying pan, and fry the *tortillas* for 30 seconds on each side. Drain on absorbent kitchen paper and keep warm. Heat the butter in the pan, and fry the onion, chilli, *epazote* or coriander, tomato and chopped flowers or spinach for 3 minutes. Add the salt, pepper and single cream, and simmer for 5 minutes.

■ Grease a round 20 cm (8 inch) ovenproof dish and place four *tortillas* in it, overlapping slightly. Place half the courgette mixture on top, then spoon a quarter of the soured cream over it, followed by half the grated Cheddar and mozzarella cheeses. Repeat with a second layer, finishing with cheese, and reserving the rest of the soured cream for garnish. Pour over the beaten eggs, ensuring it runs down the sides. Bake in the oven at 180°C, 350°F, Gas Mark 4 for about 30 minutes. Spoon the remainder of the soured cream over the top. Sprinkle with salt and garnish with more blossoms or parsley sprigs.

151

Budin de Espinaca

SPINACH AND POTATO CASSEROLE

SERVES 4

This is a tasty dish with a fancy presentation. I love spinach, apart from its nutritional value. This dish goes extremely well with fish dishes. I found it in my grandmother's cookery book; I hope you, too, will enjoy it.

INGREDIENTS

oil	1 egg, separated
2 tablespoons fine breadcrumbs	450 g (1 lb) fresh spinach
450 g (1 lb) potatoes, cooked and mashed	1/2 onion, finely chopped
3 tablespoons grated *queso de Chihuahua* or mature Cheddar cheese	1 tablespoon tomato purée
75 g (3 oz) butter	1 green chilli, finely chopped
1/2 teaspoon salt	pinch of grated nutmeg
1/4 teaspoon ground black pepper	

METHOD

■ Brush the inside of an ovenproof dish with oil and sprinkle with the breadcrumbs. Mix the mashed potatoes with the grated cheese, butter, salt, pepper and beaten egg yolk. Line the dish with this mixture.

■ Wash the spinach thoroughly, removing any tough stalks, and place in a saucepan with only the water clinging to the leaves. Cover tightly and simmer for 10 minutes. Drain the spinach and cool slightly, then squeeze it in your hands to get rid of all surplus water. Chop the spinach finely.

■ Heat 2 teaspoons oil in a frying pan, and fry the onion until soft. Add the tomato purée, chopped spinach and green chilli, and simmer gently for 5 minutes. Remove from the heat and cool. Whisk the egg white until stiff, then blend into the spinach mixture with the nutmeg. Pour this mixture over the mashed potatoes and bake in the oven at 180°C, 350°F, Gas Mark 4 for 20 minutes. Serve hot.

Budin Bonampak

PLANTAIN CASSEROLE

SERVES 4

Bonampak is located south-east of Mexico City. It is rich in vegetation and bananas of all types grow in abundance. This casserole made with plantains (large bananas that cannot be eaten raw) has a sweet flavour similar to that of parsnips and makes a good vegetable side dish for pork, lamb and hot chilli dishes. Plantains are commonly found in West Indian shops.

INGREDIENTS

2 very ripe plantains, unpeeled and quartered

600 ml (1 pint) water

150 g (5 oz) butter

1¹⁄₂ teaspoons baking powder

1 tablespoon caster sugar

75 ml (3 fl oz) single cream

¹⁄₂ teaspoon ground cinnamon

METHOD

■ Boil the quartered plantains in the water for about 30 minutes or until completely soft. Drain, peel and remove the centre veins from the plantain pieces. Combine the plantain with the remaining ingredients (reserving a little cinnamon for garnish) and mash to a purée. Grease a 20 cm (8 inch) ovenproof casserole, and spoon the plantain purée in to it. Bake in the oven at 180°C, 350°F, Gas Mark 4 for about 30 minutes. Sprinkle over the reserved cinnamon and serve hot.

Budín de Camote

SWEET POTATO PURÊE

SERVES 4

*C*amote (sweet potato) is a root vegetable, with either a purple skin and white flesh or ochre skin and yellow flesh. It is sweet-flavoured, has a texture similar to that of potato, and must always be eaten cooked. It can be boiled in its skin, then peeled and mashed, or cut into thick slices and fried in a little butter. Alternatively, it can be baked in its 'jacket' like a potato, but remember that, unlike the potato, the skin of the *camote* is not edible.

In the United States, it is customary to eat sweet potato at Thanksgiving dinners. In Mexico, it is popular both as a vegetable and as a dessert, when sugar and fruit flavours are added to it. Sweet potatoes can be found in the UK at West Indian shops, as well as at some of the larger supermarkets. This recipe is for a side dish.

INGREDIENTS

450 g (1 lb) sweet potato	65 g (2½ oz) butter
600 ml (1 pint) water	150 ml (¼ pint) double cream
1 teaspoon baking powder	1 tablespoon breadcrumbs

METHOD

■ Boil the sweet potato in the water for 35 minutes or until tender. Peel off the skin and mash to a purée while still hot. Stir in the baking powder, butter and cream. Turn the mixture into a well greased ovenproof dish and bake in the oven at 180°C, 350°F, Gas Mark 4 for 20 minutes. Spread the breadcrumbs on the top and bake for another 10 minutes. Serve hot.

Calabacitas con Elote

COURGETTES AND CORN IN TOMATO SAUCE

SERVES 4

Courgettes form almost a basic diet in Mexico. We add them to *molli* sauces, to cream sauces, and to tomato sauces, and we enjoy them just with butter and black pepper. Courgettes are very delicate in flavour and must never be overcooked. It is also important to use them soon after they have been cut or bought, to avoid letting them get bitter. Dark green, firm courgettes are the best ones to choose when shopping. If you cut them from the garden, then the smaller and lighter in colour they are the better, but these don't keep. This is a good side dish.

INGREDIENTS

4 ripe tomatoes, charred and peeled (see page 43)	100 ml (4 fl oz) water
$^1/_2$ green chilli, charred (see page 42)	4 courgettes, cubed
1 clove garlic, charred (see page 43)	100 g (4 oz) fresh or frozen corn kernels
$^1/_2$ onion, charred (see page 43)	$^1/_4$ teaspoon salt
2 teaspoons oil	pinch of ground black pepper

METHOD

■ Place the tomatoes, chilli, garlic and onion in a blender and blend to a purée. Heat the oil in a saucepan and fry the purée for 3 minutes, stirring continually. Add the water, courgettes, corn, salt and pepper, and simmer for about 10 minutes. Serve hot.

Chiles en Nogada

STUFFED PEPPERS WITH WALNUT SAUCE

SERVES 4

I remember as a child running to my mother for money to buy *una docena* (one dozen) walnuts. The seller carried them on his back in a hessian sack and shouted as he walked along the street: 'Nueces de Castilla, Nueces' (nuts from Castille), distinguishing them from the native pecan nuts.

Chiles en Nogada has a short season, from the end of August to 15th and 16th September, the Mexican Independence celebration, because the walnuts have to be green enough to enable the cook to peel off their fine, somewhat bitter skin. With its garnish of red pomegranate seeds sprinkled on a snow white, creamy, nut sauce over the deep green *chiles poblanos*, the dish displays the colours of the Mexican flag.

The name *nogada* derives from *nuez*, meaning, in this case, green walnuts which have been peeled and ground. I use ground almonds which make life easier and offer just as good a flavour the whole year round. The dish can be served as a starter, a side dish for a cold buffet, or as a main course with beans and rice. It is served at room temperature and can be prepared ahead of time.

INGREDIENTS

PICADILLO

100 g (4 oz) minced beef

100 g (4 oz) minced pork

2 teaspoons vinegar

$^1/_4$ teaspoon salt

$^1/_4$ teaspoon ground black pepper

$^1/_4$ teaspoon sugar

1 tablespoon oil

$^1/_2$ onion, finely chopped

1 clove garlic, crushed

2 green chillies, chopped

1 red pepper, deseeded and cubed

2 sticks celery, sliced

9 stuffed green olives, sliced

1 teaspoon flaked almonds

1 tablespoon raisins

3 tablespoons tomato purée

250 ml (8 fl oz) water

PEPPERS

4 medium-sized green *poblano* or green peppers

1 small lettuce, shredded

seeds from 1 pomegranate or 100 g (4 oz) cubed red pepper, to garnish

SAUCE

50 g (2 oz) ground almonds

150 ml ($^1/_4$ pint) soured cream

4 tablespoons cream cheese

$^1/_2$ teaspoon lemon juice

$^1/_4$ teaspoon salt

METHOD

■ To make the filling, mix the meats together and season with the vinegar, salt, pepper and sugar. Heat the oil in a frying pan, and fry the onion, garlic, chillies, red pepper and celery for 3 minutes. Add the meat and stir over high heat for about 10 minutes or until it starts to brown and the liquid is absorbed. Discard any surplus oil, add the remaining filling ingredients, and simmer for 15 minutes or until the mixture starts to dry, stirring occasionally. Allow to cool.

■ Meanwhile, char the skins of the green peppers on a very hot griddle or in a very hot heavy-based frying pan, turning frequently, until the skins blister. Put the peppers inside a polythene bag, seal the bag and set aside for 10 minutes. (This enhances the flavour of the peppers, while it cooks them further and allows the skins to be peeled off easily). Remove the peppers from the bag and peel off as much skin as possible. Cut a slit in the side of each pepper and remove the seeds. Stuff the peppers with the cool filling. (Alternatively, cut the stems and tops off the peppers and remove the seeds that way.)

■ Place the stuffed peppers on a bed of shredded lettuce in a serving dish. (They look pretty with the slits uppermost). For the sauce, mix the almonds, soured cream, cream cheese, lemon juice and salt, and spoon over the peppers. Garnish with the pomegranate seeds or red pepper pieces.

VARIATION

For smaller portions, stuff the peppers and cut them in half lengthways, then garnish.

Cebollitas Asadas

GRILLED SPRING ONIONS

SERVES 4

Suitable for a barbecue, and delicious when eaten with *fajitas* or *Tacos al Carbón*, yet very simple to do.

INGREDIENTS

8 spring onions	salt and ground black pepper
¹/₂ lime or lemon	

METHOD

■ If you are barbecuing, place the spring onions on the same grill 3 minutes before the other things are ready, turning them to achieve an even brown colour. Sprinkle them with lime, salt and pepper and eat hot. Otherwise, heat them on a dry griddle or in a heavy-based frying pan until limp. Season and serve.

Chiles Rellenos de Guacamole

PEPPERS STUFFED WITH AVOCADO

꒰Ꙭ꒱

SERVES 8

Chiles Rellenos are so popular in Mexico that almost every experienced cook creates her own version. Here is a simple, tasty recipe that can be served cold accompanied by either warm corn *tortillas* or *totopos* (see pages 24 and 46).

INGREDIENTS

8 green *poblano* or green peppers	4 green chillies, finely chopped
600 ml (1 pint) distilled vinegar	4 spring onions, finely chopped
salt	1/4 teaspoon ground black pepper
600 ml (1 pint) water	juice of 1 lime
1 onion, sliced	4 ripe avocados
4 ripe tomatoes, finely chopped	1 tablespoon olive oil
8 sprigs fresh coriander, finely chopped	1/2 teaspoon dried mixed herbs, to garnish

METHOD

■ Char the skins of the peppers by placing them on a very hot griddle or in a very hot heavy-based frying pan, turning them frequently, until the skins are blistered. Put them inside a polythene bag, seal the bag and set aside for 10 minutes. (This enhances the flavour of the peppers while it cooks them further and allows the skins to be peeled off easily). Remove the peppers from the bag and peel off as much skin as possible. Cut a slit in the side of each one, remove the seeds, and put the peppers in a non-metallic bowl. Add the vinegar, 1/2 teaspoon, salt, the water and onion rings, and leave to marinate for about 2 hours.

■ In a separate bowl, mix the tomatoes, coriander, chillies, spring onions, 1/4 teaspoon salt, the black pepper and lime juice. Just before serving, drain the peppers, reserving the onions. Halve, stone, peel and mash the avocados, and mix with the vegetables. Stuff the peppers with the avocado mixture and place on a bed of lettuce. Sprinkle the olive oil over them and garnish with the reserved onion rings and the mixed herbs.

Chiles Rellenos de Queso

──────── CHEESE-STUFFED PEPPERS WITH TOMATO SAUCE ────────

SERVES 6

Chiles Rellenos are a traditional Mexican dish. The peppers can be stuffed with anything you like – vegetables, cheese, fruit, fish, cooked meats – and can be coated with egg or vinaigrette, and served with almond or tomato sauce. They are eaten up and down the country and enjoyed by all. Serve them with warm corn or flour *tortillas*. If you are serving several other things, then cut the peppers in half lengthways once they are cooked as they look more attractive. In Mexico, the peppers traditionally used are *chiles poblanos* which are large, hot and very dark green. However you can use green peppers and make the sauce hotter. It is amazing how even Mexicans ask me where I bought the *poblanos* when all they have eaten have been green peppers.

INGREDIENTS

6 *poblano* or green peppers, 9–10 cm (3¹/₂–4 inches) long

200 g (8 oz) mature Cheddar cheese, grated

3 large eggs, separated

2 tablespoons plain flour

oil for deep-frying

1 quantity *Salsa para Enchiladas* (see page 35) made extra hot

METHOD

■ Scorch the skins of the peppers by placing them on a very hot griddle or in a very hot heavy-based frying pan, turning them frequently, until the skins are blistered. Put them inside a polythene bag, seal the bag and set aside for 10 minutes. (This enhances the flavour of the peppers while it cooks them further and allows the skins to be peeled off easily). Remove the peppers from the bag and peel off as much skin as possible. Cut a slit in the side of each pepper and remove the seeds. (Alternatively, cut off the stems and tops of the peppers and remove the seeds that way).

■ Stuff each pepper with grated cheese, reserving a small amount for garnish. Hold the openings together and secure with cocktail sticks. If the pepper breaks anywhere else, fasten it together with more cocktail sticks.

■ Beat the egg whites until they are stiff. In a separate bowl, beat the yolks until they are fluffy and pale in colour. Combine the two by gently folding the yolk into the white. Heat about 5 cm (2 inches) oil in a deep frying pan. Toss one pepper at a time in the flour, and then in the egg batter. Carefully place it in the hot oil, keeping the heat low as the egg burns easily. Using a kitchen fork and spoon, carefully turn the pepper over until it is golden brown all over. Remove it from the oil and drain on absorbent kitchen paper. Repeat until all the peppers are fried. When cool enough, carefully search the peppers for the cocktail sticks by applying gentle pressure to different parts of the pepper with your fingers. Remove and discard the cocktail sticks.

■ Spread some of the tomato sauce in the bottom of an ovenproof dish and place the fried peppers on top. Pour the rest of the sauce over the peppers and cover the dish with kitchen foil. Bake in the oven at 180°C, 350°F, Gas Mark 4 for about 45 minutes, then uncover the peppers, sprinkle with the reserved cheese, and cook for another 10 minutes. Serve with white rice, beans and lots of warm *tortillas*.

Coliflor Capeada

——————— CAULIFLOWER FRITTERS IN TOMATO SAUCE ———————

SERVES 4

Capeada means 'coated in egg and fried'. This is a most tasty way of eating cauliflower, ideal with any of the meat dishes or as a vegetarian main course with rice and beans.

INGREDIENTS

150 ml (¼ pint) water	oil
¼ teaspoon salt	4 tablespoons plain flour
1 small cauliflower, quartered	½ quantity *Salsa para Enchiladas* (see page 35)
100 g (4 oz) Cheddar cheese, cut into wedges	2 tablespoons grated Cheddar cheese
2 eggs, separated	

METHOD

■ Put the water in a saucepan, add the salt and bring to the boil. Add the cauliflower and cook for 10 minutes. Drain and cool. Using a sharp knife, make an incision about 5 cm (2 inches) deep half way down each cauliflower quarter, without cutting all the way through. Insert a wedge of cheese in each slit and secure with cocktail sticks.

■ Beat the egg yolks until they are pale in colour. In a separate bowl, whisk the egg whites until they form peaks. Carefully fold the egg yolk into the white. Heat some oil in a deep frying pan. Dip the cauliflower first into the flour, then into the egg batter, then fry in the hot oil on both sides until golden. Drain on absorbent kitchen paper and, when cool enough to handle, remove and discard the cocktail sticks. Put the cauliflower pieces in an ovenproof dish.

■ Bring the sauce to the boil, pour it over the cauliflower and sprinkle with the grated cheese. Bake in the oven at 180°C, 350°F, Gas Mark 4 for 30 minutes. Serve hot.

Elotes Asados

BARBECUED CORN ON THE COB

SERVES 4

This is a very easy way to cook and eat corn on the cob. The cobs are cooked in their green leaf wrapping. The roasting dries the kernels and concentrates the flavour, making the corn taste nutty.

INGREDIENTS

4 fresh corn on the cob	salt
40 g (1¹/₂ oz) butter, melted	cayenne pepper
2 lemons	

METHOD

■ Using a sharp knife, cut along the length of each of the cobs, cutting through the leaves. Open carefully and brush the kernels with melted butter. Cook on a barbecue for 25–45 minutes, turning frequently and allowing them to burn slightly. Peel back the leaves and squeeze half a lemon over each cob. Sprinkle with salt and cayenne, and eat hot.

VARIATION

If the weather does not permit you to barbecue, then proceed as above and roast the corn in the oven at 200°C, 400°F, Gas Mark 6 for 40–50 minutes.

Crepas de Cuitlacoche

———— PANCAKES FILLED WITH *CUITLACOCHE* ————

᷍ᴧᴧᴧ᷍

MAKES 6–12 crêpes

Like truffles, this delicacy has been popular since ancient times. *Cuitlacoche* is a fungus which develops on corn cobs, deforming the kernels by causing them to swell up and turn black. It is similar to wild mushrooms in colour, texture and flavour. The natives have always used it as a filling for *quesadillas* or *tacos,* and it is now a sign of refinement to serve *cuitlacoche* as a filling for crêpes. In Mexico, *cuitlacoche* is also available in cans.

This light and unusual dish makes an excellent starter, served with soured cream. The crêpes are prepared at least 2 hours in advance, and the filling can be made at the same time, then the dish assembled just before required.

INGREDIENTS

CRÊPES

275 g (10 oz) plain flour

¹/₂ teaspoon baking powder

¹/₂ teaspoon salt

2 medium eggs

600 ml (1 pint) milk

2 tablespoons oil

oil for cooking

FILLING

1 teaspoon oil

¹/₂ onion, charred and finely chopped (see page 43)

1 clove garlic, charred and finely chopped (see page 43)

275 g (10 oz) *cuitlacoche* or mushrooms, chopped

1 green chilli, finely chopped

3 leaves fresh *epazote* or coriander, chopped

¹/₄ teaspoon salt

SAUCE

2 tablespoons milk

150 ml (¹/₄ pint) soured cream

METHOD

■ To make the crêpes, place the dry ingredients in a mixing bowl, make a well in the centre and add the eggs and a little milk. Beat together, gradually blending in the flour. Beat until smooth, then gradually beat in the remaining milk and the oil. Cover and chill for at least 2 hours.

■ Brush a small heavy-based frying pan, about 15 cm (6 inches) in diameter, with oil, and heat thoroughly. Add about 2 tablespoons crêpe batter, tilting the pan so that it covers the base thinly. Pour any surplus batter remaining on the surface straight back into the bowl before it sets. Cook for about 1 minute over medium heat, using a spatula to release the crêpe from the sides of the pan, and shaking the pan a little to prevent it sticking. When the crêpe is golden brown on the underside, toss or turn it, and cook for another 30 seconds. Slide it on to a plate and cover it with another plate, upside-down. Continue in this manner until the batter is finished.

■ To make the filling, heat the oil in a heavy-based frying pan, and fry the onion and garlic until golden. Add the *cuitlacoche* or mushrooms, chilli, *epazote* or coriander and salt, and cook for about 5 minutes, stirring occasionally.

■ Grease an ovenproof dish with butter. Fill each crêpe with 1 tablespoon *cuitlacoche* mixture, roll up and place in the prepared dish. When all the crêpes have been filled, cover the dish tightly with kitchen foil and bake in the oven at 180°C, 350°F, Gas Mark 4 for 15–20 minutes or until warmed through.

■ Meanwhile, mix the milk with the soured cream. Remove the crêpes from the oven, spoon over the soured cream sauce, and serve immediately.

Esquites

FRIED SWEETCORN AND MUSHROOMS

SERVES 4

Fresh or frozen corn kernels can be used for this tasty side dish. The flavouring traditionally comes from *epazote*, but if this is not available, fresh coriander is a good substitute. It makes a good vegetarian filling for *fajitas* or soft *tacos*.

INGREDIENTS

2 tablespoons oil	350 g (12 oz) fresh or frozen corn kernels
½ onion, finely chopped	100 g (4 oz) mushrooms, sliced
1 red pepper, deseeded and sliced	¼ teaspoon salt
4 tablespoons finely chopped fresh *epazote* or coriander	¼ teaspoon ground black pepper
2 green chillies, thinly sliced	1 teaspoon lime or lemon juice

METHOD

■ Heat the oil in a frying pan, and fry the onion, red pepper, *epazote* or coriander and chillies for 3 minutes. Stir in the corn kernels, mushrooms, salt and pepper. Cover and cook over medium heat for 5 minutes. Uncover and continue cooking, stirring occasionally, for another 3 minutes. Mix in the lime or lemon juice, and serve hot.

Lentejas en Adobo

LENTILS IN CHILLI SAUCE

SERVES 4

Lentils are full of goodness and this nutritious dish can be considered a meal in one as it also includes meat. It goes well with rice and soft warm *tortillas*. It is a versatile dish – you can omit the *ancho* chillies, or turn it into a vegetarian dish by omitting the meat, and still have a very tasty result.

INGREDIENTS

225 g (8 oz) lentils	1 bay leaf
225 g (8 oz) stewing pork, cubed (optional)	2 ancho chillies
1 teaspoon malt vinegar	1 tablespoon tomato purée
$^1/_2$ teaspoon salt	$^1/_2$ teaspoon dried oregano
$^1/_2$ teaspoon ground black pepper	$^1/_2$ teaspoon ground cloves
1 ripe plantain, unpeeled and cut into 2.5 cm (1 inch) rounds	$^1/_4$ teaspoon ground cinnamon
	1 clove garlic
1 onion, chopped	2 tablespoons oil
1 chicken stock cube, crumbled	1 fresh or canned pineapple slice, roughly chopped
1 litre (1$^3/_4$ pints) water	

METHOD

■ Pick over the lentils and remove any unwanted bits and small stones. Rinse the lentils under cold running water, and place them in a large saucepan with the meat (if using), vinegar, salt, half the black pepper, the plantain, onion, stock cube, water and bay leaf. Cover and simmer for 30–45 minutes or until the meat is tender and the lentils and plantain are soft. Remove the plantain pieces and peel off the skin.

■ Heat the chillies in a dry frying pan until soft. Discard the stems and seeds, and soak the chillies in 150 ml ($^1/_4$ pint) of the liquid from the lentils. Put the chillies and their liquid in a blender with the tomato purée, oregano, cloves, remaining black pepper, cinnamon and garlic, and work to a smooth paste. Heat the oil in a large flameproof casserole, and fry the chilli paste for 5 minutes, stirring occasionally, then add the lentils, meat, plantain and chopped pineapple. Cover and simmer for 30 minutes. Serve hot.

Plátano Macho Frito

FRIED PLANTAIN

SERVES 4

The flavour of plantain is similar to that of banana but a little sweeter. When fried, plantain does not fall apart like a fried sliced banana would. It goes extremely well with rice.

INGREDIENTS

2 very ripe but firm plantains	75 g (3 oz) butter

METHOD

■ Put the whole plantains on the work surface and roll them backwards and forwards a few times with the palms of your hands as if they were a rolling pin. This enhances the flavour. To peel the plantains, cut them in half and slit the skins lengthways. Remove the plantain flesh, retaining the skin. Slice each half plantain lengthways into four slices.

■ Heat the butter in a frying pan, and fry the plantain slices for about 4 minutes on each side or until golden. As the plantain slices turn golden, remove them from the pan and put them back into their skins to keep warm. Plantain does not keep or reheat well so eat it immediately.

Quelites con Jitomate

GREENS WITH TOMATOES

SERVES 4

Quelites encompasses all manner of 'greens', like beetroot tops, spinach, Swiss chard and other types of green leaves that can be found in the wild. They are also used as a filling for *tacos* but they must be piquant.

INGREDIENTS

450 g (1 lb) spinach	2 chillies, charred (see page 42)
100 ml (4 fl oz) water	1 tablespoon oil
4 ripe tomatoes, charred and peeled (see page 43)	pinch of salt
1 onion, charred (see page 43)	pinch of ground black pepper
2 garlic cloves, charred (see page 43)	

METHOD ■ Wash the spinach and parboil it in a covered saucepan with only the water clinging to its leaves for 10 minutes. Drain it and press out as much water as possible by squeezing it gently with the back of a spoon. Chop the spinach finely. Put the water, tomatoes, onion, garlic and chillies in a blender and work to a purée. Heat the oil in a frying pan, and fry the tomato purée for 5 minutes. Add the chopped spinach, salt and black pepper, and simmer for another 5 minutes. Serve hot.

Romeritos

GREENS WITH DRIED SHRIMP FRITTERS IN *MOLE* SAUCE

SERVES 4 *R*evoltijo or *romeritos* are the names given to this dish, which is mainly enjoyed on days, such as Christmas and Easter, when meat should not be eaten. I have never seen *romeritos* grow anywhere but in Mexico. It looks like very fine chives but is darker green in colour with no particular taste. Cooked spinach, finely shredded, can be used instead. The ingredients must all be cooked separately and assembled at the last minute. Eight freshly cooked prawns may be used instead of the fritters if you prefer to keep the calories under control.

INGREDIENTS

450 g (1 lb) *romeritos* or finely shredded cooked spinach	1 quantity *Salsa Adobada* (see page 36)
275 g (10 oz) canned *nopales* (see page 173)	shrimp fritters (see page 115) or 12 freshly cooked prawns
12 baby potatoes, cooked, peeled and halved	

METHOD ■ Put the *romeritos* or spinach in a saucepan with the *nopales*, potatoes and *Salsa*, and heat through thoroughly. Add the shrimp fritters or prawns, and simmer for a few minutes. Garnish with shrimps or prawns and serve with *Arroz Blanco* (see page 98) and warm corn *tortillas*.

Rajas de Chile Poblano

PEPPER STRIPS IN HOT TOMATO SAUCE

SERVES 4

Rajas make an excellent filling for vegetarian *fajitas*, or warm corn *tortilla tacos*. Different types of green chilli are used in Mexico and this is a popular typical recipe which does not lose too much authenticity by being made with green peppers instead of *poblano*. This is a starter or side dish which goes well with grilled steak.

INGREDIENTS

1 tablespoon oil	1 tablespoon chopped fresh *epazote* or coriander
1 large onion, finely sliced	
2 large *poblanos* or green peppers, deseeded and finely sliced	2 tablespoons tomato purée
	100 ml (4 fl oz) water
2 green chillies, sliced	4 tablespoons soured cream
¹⁄₄ teaspoon salt	50 g (2 oz) Cheddar cheese, grated, to garnish
¹⁄₄ teaspoon ground black pepper	
¹⁄₄ teaspoon sugar	

METHOD

■ Heat the oil in a heavy-based frying pan, and sauté the onion, peppers and chillies. Add the remaining ingredients, except the cream and cheese, stir, cover tightly, and simmer for about 5 minutes. Stir in the cream and garnish with the cheese.

■ Serve hot with warm corn or flour *tortillas*. Let each person make his or her own soft *tacos* by putting a *tortilla* on a plate, spreading a tablespoon of filling along the middle, and then rolling up and eating it, holding the *taco* in the right hand, between the thumb and three fingers. Allow the little finger to go underneath the end of the *taco* and tilt it up, thus preventing the filling from escaping at the other end.

Ensalada De Jícama

YAM BEAN SALAD

SERVES 4

Jícama (or yam bean) belongs to the Leguminosae family which produces edible tubers. Despite this, its protein content is low and its popularity is due to its whiteness and its juicy texture. *Jícama* is native to Mexico and grows profusely. It has a thick, brown, unattractive skin which is easily peeled back and can be bought in Mexican markets at any time of the year. I have seen it occasionally in this country in Chinese supermarkets and it is well worth trying to find it, especially for an outdoor barbecue. It should be eaten by hand and by the slice, each about 10 cm (5 inches) in diameter. If this is too daunting, then cut it into manageable pieces. It is a good weight-watcher's stand by.

INGREDIENTS

2 medium-sized *jícamas*	juice of 1 lime
1 red pepper, deseeded and sliced	$^1/_2$ teaspoon cayenne pepper
2 tablespoons unsalted peanuts	$^1/_2$ teaspoon salt

METHOD

■ Peel the *jícama* and rinse it under cold running water. Cut it into 1 cm ($^1/_2$ inch) strips and arrange in a bowl. Mix the pepper, peanuts, lime juice, cayenne and salt, and sprinkle over the *jícama*, taking care it covers all the pieces. Chill until required.

Cocktail de Aguacate

—— AVOCADO COCKTAIL ——

SERVES 6

This makes an excellent vegetarian starter. The sauce can be made well in advance and stored in the refrigerator.

INGREDIENTS

8 tablespoons tomato ketchup	$^1/_4$ teaspoon ground black pepper
100 g (4 oz) cream cheese	2 ripe avocados
juice of 1 lime or lemon	$^1/_2$ Webb's lettuce, finely shredded
$^1/_4$ teaspoon vegetarian Worcestershire sauce	4 spring onions, finely chopped, to garnish
$^1/_4$ teaspoon Tabasco sauce	

METHOD

■ Mix all the ingredients together, except the avocados, lettuce and spring onions. Cover and chill the sauce in the refrigerator for at least 1 hour. Just before serving, halve and stone each avocado, then slice into eight. Remove the peel without breaking the slices. (It is easier to work this way rather than peeling first.) Divide the shredded lettuce between individual cocktail glasses, lay the avocado slices on top, and spoon the sauce over. Serve chilled, garnished with chopped spring onions.

Ensalada Navidena

————— CHRISTMAS SALAD —————

SERVES 4

This is an unusual salad, both in colour and in the combination and texture of its ingredients. The *jícama* (see pages 170–171) is especially exotic to British palates. The salad is usually prepared for Christmas Eve, when it adds a special touch of colour to the meal.

INGREDIENTS

¹/₂ Webb's lettuce, very finely shredded	3 tablespoons unsalted peanuts
4 small cooked beetroots, peeled and thinly sliced	1 tablespoon pine kernels or flaked almonds
1 large orange, peeled and thinly sliced	juice of 1 lemon
1 eating apple, cored and thinly sliced	150 ml (¹/₂ pint) sweet sherry
2 ripe bananas, sliced	¹/₂ teaspoon salt
1 *jícama*, peeled, sliced and cut into bite-sized pieces	cayenne pepper

METHOD

■ Arrange a bed of lettuce on a flat serving dish, then arrange all the vegetables and fruits in circles of colour on top of the lettuce. Scatter over the peanuts and pine kernels or flaked almonds. Just before serving, mix the lemon juice with the sherry and salt, and spoon over the salad. Finish with a sprinkling of cayenne.

VARIATION

If you cannot find *jícama*, this salad can be made with cauliflower florets.

Ensalada De Nopalitos

PADDLE CACTUS SALAD

SERVES 4

*N*opalitos are the most original vegetable in the Mexican diet. They are the tender, oval, fleshy paddles of the prickly pear cactus plant. In Mexican markets *nopalitos* can be bought with the sharp thorns already cut off and, when prepared, they make a most eye-catching dish. Older, darker paddle leaves are not suitable for human consumption because they are very fibrous and impossible to chew.

Canned *Nopales al Natural* can occasionally be found in speciality shops in Britain but French beans may be used as a substitute. This is a good side dish or filling for warm soft *tortillas*. Preparation takes about 3 hours.

INGREDIENTS

275 g (10 oz) fresh or canned *nopales*, or cooked French beans	1 tablespoon olive oil
1 litre (1³/₄ pints) water	¹/₂ teaspoon dried oregano
salt	¹/₂ teaspoon ground black pepper
pinch of bicarbonate of soda	2 large ripe tomatoes, sliced
4 tablespoons chopped fresh coriander	1 onion, thinly sliced
2 green chillies, sliced	2 tablespoons white crumbly cheese, such as white Cheshire, finely crumbled
3 tablespoons lime or lemon juice	

METHOD

■ If you are able to obtain the fresh paddles, first remove the thorns. Hold each paddle by the base and, with a sharp knife, slice off the thorns, ensuring none are left. This is quite easy because when the paddles are young and tender, the thorns are hardly formed. The remaining skin in between the thorns does not need to be removed. Wash the paddles and cut them into 1 cm (¹/₂ inch) squares. Soak them in half the water with 2 table-spoons salt added for about 3 hours or until all the slimy substance is released. Drain and wash under cold running water.

■ Place the *nopales* in a saucepan with the remaining water and the bicarbonate of soda. Simmer for about 20 minutes or until tender, skimming frequently. Drain, cool and place in a salad bowl. Add the coriander, chillies, lime or lemon juice, olive oil, oregano, ¹/₂ teaspoon salt and the pepper, and mix well. Arrange the tomato slices and onion rings on top, and sprinkle with cheese. Serve cold, with warm *tortillas*.

Escabeche de Verduras

VEGETABLE *ESCABECHE*

SERVES 6

This is a cooked vegetable salad. The more popular varieties of this same dish include shellfish, cooked chicken or cooked meats. It is a good lunch or side dish.

INGREDIENTS

4 tablespoons olive oil	1 green pepper, deseeded and sliced
4 carrots, sliced	1 red pepper, deseeded and sliced
4 spring onions, roughly chopped	1 bay leaf
200 g (7 oz) cauliflower florets	1/2 teaspoon salt
200 g (7 oz) runner beans, sliced	1/2 teaspoon ground black pepper
200 g (7 oz) shelled peas	1/2 teaspoon dried oregano
200 g (7 oz) corn kernels	16 stuffed green olives
2 fresh chillies or canned *jalapeños*, sliced	250 ml (8 fl oz) vinegar
2 cloves garlic, crushed	pinch of sugar

METHOD

■ Heat the oil in a heavy-based frying pan, and sauté all the vegetables until limp. Add the bay leaf, salt, black pepper, oregano, olives, vinegar and sugar, and bring to the boil. Cover, remove from the heat and leave to cool. When cool, refrigerate until required.

Pico De Gallo

FRUIT AND VEGETABLE SALAD

SERVES 6

Pico de Gallo is the name given to any salad which is coarsely chopped, resembling food for chickens! Any combination of raw vegetables is good, but, of course, *jícama*, and assorted fruits are a must. This traditional way of eating cucumber, *jícama*, radishes, orange, carrots, peppers, fresh pineapple and strawberries is now favoured at social occasions because it can be offered with drinks and is low in calories.

INGREDIENTS

¹/₂ cucumber, peeled and cut into small sticks	¹/₂ fresh pineapple, peeled and roughly chopped
1 large *jicama*, cut into 2.5 cm (1 inch) sticks	10 radishes, sliced and cut into flower shapes
1 orange, peeled and segmented	juice of 1 lemon
1 green pepper, deseeded and thinly sliced	salt
1 red pepper, deseeded and thinly sliced	cayenne pepper

METHOD

■ Arrange all the vegetables and fruits in a serving dish. Just before serving, sprinkle with lemon juice, salt and cayenne. Serve immediately.

Ensalada Tenango

AVOCADO AND TOMATO SALAD

SERVES 4

Avocados feature strongly in the Mexican kitchen. This is a tasty way of eating them.

INGREDIENTS

3 tablespoons oil	DRESSING
2 corn *tortillas* (see page 24), cut into very thin strips	juice of 1 lemon
2 ripe avocados, stoned, peeled and sliced	2 tablespoons olive oil
2 large ripe tomatoes, sliced	¹/₂ teaspoon salt
1 tablespoon chopped fresh coriander	¹/₄ teaspoon ground black pepper
¹/₂ onion, finely sliced	pinch of dried oregano

METHOD

■ Heat the oil in a frying pan, and fry the *tortilla* strips just until they go golden. Drain on absorbent kitchen paper.

■ Arrange the avocado and tomato slices alternately on a serving plate. Top with the coriander and onion rings. For the dressing, whisk together the lemon juice, olive oil, salt, pepper and oregano, and pour it over the salad. Just before serving, garnish it with the fried *tortilla* strips.

Jalapeños En Vinagre

PICKLED *JALAPEÑO* CHILLIES

MAKES 750 ml
(1¼ pints)

This appetising pickle is deceptively hot! It goes well with beans, rice, *tortas*, *empanadas*, *quesadillas* and all *antojitos*. It is a good condiment to have on the table for those who like very hot food. It keeps for weeks. Be sure to slice the chillies with a knife and fork on absorbent kitchen paper to avoid getting 'hot fingers' which may irritate sensitive skin.

INGREDIENTS

4 tablespoons oil	¼ teaspoon dried thyme
12 fresh *jalapeño* chillies (or 24 small green chillies), sliced	¼ teaspoon ground cumin
2 large carrots, thinly sliced	¼ teaspoon aniseed
2 large onions, thinly sliced	1 tablespoon salt
½ medium cauliflower, separated into florets	1 teaspoon ground black pepper
1 red pepper, deseeded and thinly sliced	2 bay leaves
¼ teaspoon dried oregano	1 head of garlic, cut in half crossways
¼ teaspoon dried marjoram	1 tablespoon sugar
	1 litre (2 pints) distilled malt vinegar

METHOD

■ Heat the oil in a large saucepan, and fry the chillies and vegetables for about 2 minutes to seal them. Remove them to a mixing bowl. Add the remaining ingredients to the pan and boil for 10 minutes. Pour the boiling vinegar and spices over the fried vegetables, stir well and leave to cool. Bottle, seal and store. Refrigerate only after the jars have been opened. Keeps for up to 3 months.

OPPOSITE   Left to right: *Frijoles al Arriero* (tipsy beans, page 131) and *Esquites* (fried sweetcorn and mushrooms, page 166)

OVERLEAF   Top to bottom: *Crema de Mango* (mango cream with almonds, page 193), *Ensalada de Frutas Tropicales* (tropical fruit salad, page 192) and *Cafe de Olla* (coffee with cinnamon and brown sugar, page 196)

DESSERTS

COOKED desserts do not occupy a very prominent place in the Mexican meal, partly because fresh fruit is abundant, cheap and healthy. Fresh fruit salads, sliced fresh pineapple, watermelon, mangoes, plums, prickly pears, fresh figs, paw-paw and many other delicious fruits all militate against complicated cooked sweets.

There are some delicious native fruits which complete the kaleidoscope of the Mexican fruit market. There is *mamey, zapote chico, zapote negro, granada china, pitaya, chirimoya, guanabana* and an entire family of bananas, from the large plantain which is used for cooking to the smallest sweet Dominico, which is the size of your little finger. Many of these fruits make excellent sorbets and ice-creams which often appear on Mexican menus. Last but not least, we have to remember vanilla, which was found in Mexico and is popular the world over. In Mexico it features in many milk and egg-based favourites.

Desserts are seldom eaten hot, with the exception of *Buñuelos, Churros* and *Crepas con Cajeta.* Most desserts are served well chilled – even fruit is served chilled. Cream is not usual either, fruit salads and other fresh fruits being eaten by themselves or just with a little sugar, with the exception of strawberries. Crystallised fruits, such as pumpkin, figs, tangerines, spaghetti squash, tamarind, guava and others, are often offered after the meal.

Cakes and biscuits are becoming more popular in Mexico today, partly because of their availability in the shops, and partly because more homes have conventional ovens. Nuts, especially pecan nuts, are used in many dishes, including fruit salad. They are less oily than walnuts, smaller in size and more difficult to peel, but you can buy them ready-shelled.

With all this in mind, I have carefully chosen dessert recipes for which the ingredients are easily available and which have been my favourites over the years. I hope they become your favourite desserts, too.

Arroz con Leche

RICE PUDDING

SERVES 6

Arroz con Leche is extremely popular throughout Mexico. The rice, milk, sugar, cinnamon and eggs, which are sometimes added, are all of imported origin. Mexican rice pudding is generally sweeter than that enjoyed anywhere else. It keeps best out of the refrigerator as chilling tends to make it hard. In Mexico, long-grain rice is used, as short-grain is mostly used only for *paella*. The results are equally good with either type of rice.

INGREDIENTS

175 g (6 oz) long-grain or short-grain (pudding) rice	200 g (7 oz) sugar
450 ml (³/₄ pint) water	400 g (14 oz) can of sweetened condensed milk
450 ml (³/₄ pint) milk	3 tablespoons seedless raisins
10 cm (5 inch) cinnamon stick	3 tablespoons sultanas
3 tablespoons desiccated coconut (optional)	3 tablespoons crystallised cherries, halved
	¹/₂ teaspoon ground cinnamon

METHOD

■ Simmer the rice in the water for about 30 minutes or until very soft, adding more hot water if necessary. Add the milk, cinnamon stick, coconut if using and sugar, and continue simmering, stirring occasionally, for another 15 minutes. When the rice is ready and of a 'soupy' consistency, remove from the heat, discard the cinnamon stick and stir in the sweetened condensed milk, the raisins and sultanas. Scatter the cherries on top and sprinkle with cinnamon.

Buñuelos

CRISPY FLOUR *TORTILLAS* WITH MUSCOVADO SUGAR SYRUP

∧∨∧

SERVES 4

B*uñuelos* are very popular all over Mexico. In the south, large *buñuelos* are made using a special, complicated method. A rich dark muscovado sugar syrup is then poured over the thin, crispy *buñuelos*. In the north, they cut the flour *tortillas* into eight pieces, fry them and toss them in caster sugar and cinnamon. Prepared in this manner, they go well with coffee or chocolate. Whichever way you prefer them, they are simple to prepare provided you already have the wheat *tortillas*.

INGREDIENTS

4 wheat flour *tortillas* (see page 26)	grated rind and juice of 1 orange
oil for deep-frying	¹/₂ teaspoon aniseed
SYRUP	TO SERVE
225 g (8 oz) muscovado sugar	150 ml (¹/₄ pint) double cream
150 ml (¹/₄ pint) water	2 tablespoons chopped nuts
7.5 cm (3 inch) stick cinnamon	

METHOD

■ Heat the oil in a deep-fryer to 180°C, 350°F. For southern-style *buñuelos*, fry each whole *tortilla* in the oil for 3 minutes or until golden brown, then stand it on its side to drain on absorbent kitchen paper. For the syrup, mix the ingredients together in a saucepan and bring to the boil, stirring occasionally. Simmer over medium heat for 5 minutes, strain and then pour over the fried *tortillas* just before serving. Spoon over double cream and sprinkle with nuts.

VARIATION

If you prefer to try northern-style *buñuelos*, cut the *tortillas* into eight pieces each, and fry half of them until golden. Drain off as much oil as possible. Shake them in a brown paper bag with 100 g (4 oz) caster sugar and 2 teaspoons ground cinnamon. Repeat and eat whilst still warm. These cinnamon *buñuelos* will keep for 2–3 days in an airtight container.

Cajeta de Celaya

SOFT MILK FUDGE

SERVES 6

Cajeta de Celaya is very popular in Mexico, particularly with children, who roll it on a spoon and lick it forever. It is very sweet and equally delicious. Desserts made with it, such as *Crepas con Cajeta y Naranja* (see page 186) are also very popular. It is delicious served with vanilla ice cream, and Mexican children enjoy it also on bread and butter instead of jam.

INGREDIENTS

750 g (1¹/₂ lb) sugar	two 10 cm (5 inch) sticks cinnamon or 1 teaspoon ground cinnamon
2 litres (3¹/₂ pints) goat's or cow's milk	
¹/₂ teaspoon bicarbonate of soda	¹/₂ teaspoon vanilla essence

METHOD

■ Place all the sugar and half the milk in a 4 litre (7 pint) saucepan. Heat gently, stirring occasionally, until the sugar has dissolved then bring to the boil, reduce the heat and simmer for about 20 minutes or until the milk turns light brown. Remove from the heat. Pour the rest of the milk into another saucepan and add the bicarbonate of soda. Bring to the boil, then very gradually add to the caramel, stirring constantly with a wooden spoon. Be careful as the mixture will bubble furiously. When all the milk has been mixed in, keep stirring to ensure there are no brown sugar specks.

■ Return the pan to the heat and simmer gently for about 1¹/₂ hours, skimming off any froth that appears and stirring occasionally. Add the cinnamon and vanilla essence, and continue simmering until the temperature of the mixture reaches 120°C, 225°F. Discard the cinnamon sticks, cool and bottle. (Use the froth removed during the simmering to make *Morelianas* (see opposite).

Morelianas

FUDGE WAFERS

Morelianas are normally sold in the streets of Mexico, wrapped up in cellophane. They are about 10 cm (5 inches) in diameter and more of a confection than a dessert.

METHOD

■ All you need for this is rice paper cut into any shape you desire. When you make *cajeta* (see opposite), the recipe requires you to skim the foam that appears whilst it cooks. Collect this foam in a plate and then spread it over the rice paper while it is still warm. Cover with another layer of rice paper and leave to cool. It is now ready to eat.

Dulce de Chocolate Morelia

CHOCOLATE BLANCMANGE

MAKES 4

Mexico's desserts are almost always served refrigerated, perhaps because of the hot climate, and because they act as a cooler and palate cleanser. This dessert is so simple that it can be whisked together in minutes; in England it can even be served hot.

INGREDIENTS

600 ml (1 pint) milk	½ teaspoon ground cinnamon
175 g (6 oz) sugar	¼ teaspoon vanilla essence
3 tablespoons cornflour	2 tablespoons flaked almonds
3 tablespoons cocoa powder or 100 g (4 oz) cooking chocolate, roughly chopped	

METHOD

■ Put all the ingredients, except the nuts, in a blender and blend for 45 seconds at top speed. Pour the mixture into a saucepan and cook over low heat, stirring constantly with a wire whisk, for about 5 minutes or until it starts to thicken. Strain into a serving dish before it boils. (This must be done quickly as the mixture thickens as it cools.) Sprinkle with flaked almonds and serve hot or cold.

Chongos Zamoranos

JUNKET IN CINNAMON SYRUP

SERVES 6

Only a dessert as delicious as this could have stood the test of its odd name in Spanish – *chongos* is another name for the *chignons* in which old ladies style their hair! It is one of the three most popular desserts in Mexico, the other two being *Flan* and *Dulce de Calabaza*. Children love its sweet, chewy, squeaky texture, covered in its cinnamon-flavoured golden syrup. If you think I am exaggerating, just try it!

INGREDIENTS

2.4 litres (4 pints) milk	3 tablespoons rennet
250 g (9 oz) sugar	15 cm (6 inch) stick cinnamon
2 egg yolks (size 2)	

METHOD

■ Mix the milk, sugar and egg yolks thoroughly in a large saucepan. Warm over a low heat for about 5 minutes, stirring until it reaches body temperature (36°C, 98°F on a sugar thermometer). Mix in the rennet, cover, remove from the heat and leave in a warm place overnight.

■ The next morning, cut the curd with a knife into 4 cm (1¹/₂ inch) squares. Put a little piece of cinnamon stick into each square. Simmer, uncovered, over a very low heat for about 1 hour, increasing the heat slightly as the curd toughens. Watch that it does not boil hard or the curds will disintegrate. As the mixture warms up, the solids will separate from the buttermilk and thus boil in it. After about 4 hours, when the curds are a nice rich golden colour and the liquid has been reduced by half and is quite thick and syrupy, remove from the heat and cool. Serve chilled or at room temperature.

Cocada Con Crema

CREAM AND COCONUT DESSERT

SERVES 6

This *cocada* is very popular in my family. My grandmother used to make it, and it is light and delicious. If buying fresh coconuts, ensure that the 'eyes' are firm and fresh-looking. Shake the coconuts to ensure they contain lots of coconut water (mistakenly called 'coconut milk'). Puncture two of the black eyes and pour out and reserve the water. To separate the flesh from the husk more easily, place the whole coconut in the oven at 170°C, 325°F, Gas Mark 3 for 12–15 minutes. Then crack the husk open with a hammer and dislodge the flesh in large pieces using the tip of a strong knife. Peel off the brown skin and grate the flesh. Desiccated coconut can be used when fresh coconut is not available.

INGREDIENTS

250 g (9 oz) sugar	100 ml (4 fl oz) sherry or rum
250 ml (9 fl oz) coconut water or water	150 ml (¼ pint) double cream
225 g (8 oz) grated fresh or desiccated coconut	½ teaspoon vanilla essence
	1 tablespoon icing sugar
3 egg yolks, well beaten	2 tablespoons flaked almonds, roasted

METHOD

■ Dissolve the sugar in the water over low heat. Increase the heat and boil to the soft ball stage (115°C, 238°F). To check this without a thermometer, drop a small amount of syrup into cold water. If it can be moulded with the fingers into a soft ball, then the temperature is correct. Remove from the heat and add the coconut, beaten egg yolks and sherry. Mix well, then return to a very low heat for about 10 minutes, stirring frequently, to dry out the mixture. When you can see the bottom of the pan as you stir the spoon through the mixture, remove from the heat. Pour the mixture into a serving dish and allow to cool.

■ Whip the cream with the vanilla and icing sugar until stiff, and spoon over the cool coconut dessert. Decorate with flaked almonds and refrigerate until ready to serve.

Flan

CRÈME CARAMEL

SERVES 6

This is no ordinary crème caramel; it is an extra-delicious one. It is one of Mexico's most popular desserts – cool, smooth and sweet. Although it is often made in individual moulds, I prefer to make one large *flan* because it saves time and looks more appetising. It freezes and refrigerates extremely well.

INGREDIENTS

225 g (8 oz) sugar	300 ml ('/2 pint) milk
4 tablespoons water	3 egg yolks (size 2)
400 g (14 oz) can of sweetened condensed milk	1'/2 teaspoons vanilla essence

METHOD

■ Heat the sugar and water in a small saucepan over low heat until the sugar is dissolved. Bring to the boil, and boil, without stirring, for 8–10 minutes or until the mixture caramelises to a rich golden brown. Remove the pan from the heat, and pour the caramel into a 15 cm (6 inch) pudding basin, tipping it slowly to ensure the caramel covers the sides and bottom. Drop a little caramel on to a piece of well-buttered greaseproof paper to use as decoration.

■ Mix the milks, egg yolks and vanilla gently, but do not whip. Strain into the caramel-coated basin, cover with a clean, damp cloth and tie the cloth in place. Put the bowl in a roasting tin half-filled with warm water, allowing the edges of the cloth to touch the water, and place it in the centre of the oven at 170°C, 325°F, Gas Mark 3 for 2–2¹/₂ hours, topping up with boiling water when necessary.

■ Test the flan for readiness by piercing the centre with a knife. If it comes out clean and the custard sides have come away from the basin, uncover and cool. Refrigerate until required. To serve, run the tip of a pointed knife all around the edge of the basin and invert the *flan* on to a deep serving dish, allowing the caramel to run over the top and sides. Remove the hardened caramel from the buttered paper, break it into fine pieces and sprinkle on to the *flan*.

NOTE *Flan* can easily go wrong: If the eggs are too small the mixture will never set; if the water in the roasting tin dries up the *flan* will start baking and air bubbles will create holes in the finished flan; if the *flan* is cooked too quickly or too long, it will curdle. Despite any mishaps, however, the flavour will still be great, and don't forget that practice makes perfect.

VARIATION

For a mocha-flavoured *flan*, mix 1 tablespoon cocoa powder and 1 tablespoon Kahlua coffee liqueur into the milks and continue as directed. Just before serving, pour a little Kahlua over the top. Decorate the *flan* with fresh strawberries or pineapple slices to reduce the sweetness.

Dulce de Higo Verde

GREEN FIGS WITH CLOVES IN SYRUP

MAKES 1.2 LITRES (2 pints)

This very unusual dessert is one of my favourites. In fact, I like it so much that I have gone to the trouble of growing a fig tree in my garden, since green figs are hard to find in Britain. Fig trees in colder climates seem to bear plenty of fruit which hardly ever ripens – so this is ideal if you wish to use up your own figs!

INGREDIENTS

1.5 kg (3 lb) hard green figs	1.5 kg (3 lb) sugar
3 litres (5¼ pints) water	30 cloves

METHOD

■ Cut a cross in the head of each fig to allow the syrup to penetrate. Place all the cut figs in a saucepan, add the water, cover and simmer for 1½ hours or until the figs are very soft. Uncover and continue simmering until half the water has evaporated, skimming off the foam that appears on the surface. Add the sugar and the cloves and simmer for 30 minutes. Serve cold with cream.

Crepas con Cajeta y Naranja

—————— CRÊPES WITH FUDGE SAUCE AND ORANGE SYRUP ——————

SERVES 6

Hot desserts are unusual in Mexico (even pies are served cold), but crêpes are very popular in any of their many guises. With *cajeta*, a delicious fudge sauce, they taken on a French–Mexican flavour.

INGREDIENTS

100 g (4 oz) plain flour, sifted	2 tablespoons oil
pinch of salt	¼ quantity *Cajeta de Celaya* (see page 180)
2 eggs	225 ml (8 fl oz) orange juice
200 ml (7 fl oz) milk	2 tablespoons sugar
125 ml (4½ fl oz) warm water	8 tablespoons brandy or Cointreau

METHOD

■ To make the pancakes, put the warm water, milk, eggs, salt, flour and oil into a blender, and blend at top speed for about 1 minute. Use a spatula to dislodge any unblended flour from the blades and blend again for 5 minutes. Alternatively, place the flour and salt in a mixing bowl, make a well in the centre and add the eggs and a little milk. Beat together, gradually blending in the flour. Beat until smooth, then gradually beat in the remaining milk, the water and the oil. Cover the batter and chill for at least 2 hours.

■ Brush a 15 cm (6 inch) frying pan with a little oil and cook the crêpes as described on page 163.

■ Place the *cajeta* in the top of a double boiler, and warm it so that it spreads easily. Spread each pancake with *cajeta* and fold into four so that it is fan-shaped. Grease an ovenproof dish with a little butter and place the folded pancakes in it.

■ Put the orange juice, sugar and brandy in a saucepan, and boil together until the mixture thickens to a light syrup. Pour over the pancakes. Cover with kitchen foil and bake in the oven at 180°C, 350°F, Gas Mark 4, for 20 minutes. Serve hot.

Helado de Vainilla Con Kahlua

VANILLA ICE-CREAM WITH COFFEE LIQUEUR

MAKES about
1.7 litres
(3 pints)

Home-made ice-cream is delicious but often troublesome to make. This recipe is very easy, even children can do it, provided the tins of milk have already been boiled and cooled. It can be used as a base for any flavour of ice-cream you wish, with excellent results. It has the added advantage of being lower in cholesterol and calories because it is made with evaporated milk instead of cream and eggs. Chill all your utensils and the freezer container before use, and ensure your freezer can freeze quickly. Preparation starts 2 days before.

INGREDIENTS

400 g (14 oz) can of evaporated milk	10 tablespoons Kahlua coffee liqueur
175 g (6 oz) icing sugar	10 sponge finger biscuits or *Buñuelos* (see page 179)
½ teaspoon vanilla essence	

METHOD

■ Place the can of evaporated milk, *unopened*, in a saucepan. Cover it with water and boil for 15 minutes. Remove the can from the water and leave to cool at room temperature for about 4 hours, then refrigerate it for 24 hours, still *unopened*. (It is dangerous to open the can while it is hot.) You can boil several cans and store them, unopened, in the back of the fridge for unexpected visitors.

■ Cool all your equipment in the freezer for 10 minutes, then open the can and pour the evaporated milk into a chilled bowl. Beat with an electric mixer at top speed for 3–4 minutes or until doubled in bulk and of a whipped-egg-white consistency. Add the sugar and vanilla, and whisk just enough to blend well.

■ Pour the mixture into a chilled freezer-proof container, seal and freeze for about 5 hours. This ice-cream does not need any further whisking; it will be smooth and fluffy as it is, but it helps to put it in the refrigerator for about 30 minutes before serving to soften it a little. Pour 1 tablespoon Kahlua over each helping just before serving with sponge fingers or cinnamon *Buñuelos*.

Pan de Muerto

HALLOWE'EN BREAD

SERVES 6

This bread is traditionally made to commemorate All Saints' Day and All Souls' Day. In Mexico on these two days, graves are tended and cemeteries thoroughly spring-cleaned, turning it into a festival of flowers, beautiful scents, colour, tears, laughter and music. Candles are lit in the churches for every member of the family that has died and altars are erected in family rooms. Food, drink, flowers and *Pan de Muerto* are left among the candles and the portraits of saints and relatives, in the belief that the spirits of the dead will feast on the spirits of the food and drink.

Pan de Muerto is a round bun with dough in the shape of bones and knuckles forming a cross over the top. One round knob of dough in the middle is surrounded by small dough 'tear drops'. These are particularly tasty as they are more crispy and often have more sugar on them than the rest of the bread. *Pan de Muerto* is enjoyed in every home on or around *Dia de Muertos*, rather as Hot Cross Buns are eaten in Britain on or around Good Friday. Preparation should start the night before. It helps to warm all bowls and utensils you are going to use.

INGREDIENTS

550 g (1 lb 4 oz) strong plain flour	150 g (5 oz) butter
pinch of salt	2 eggs plus 1 egg yolk, beaten
2 tablespoons dried yeast	TOPPING
100 g (4 oz) sugar	1 egg white
1 teaspoon aniseed	50 g (2 oz) caster sugar
2 tablespoons grated orange rind	2 tablespoons pink sugar crystals (optional)
6 tablespoons water	

METHOD

■ Sift 450 (1 lb) of the flour with the salt into a mixing bowl. Mix in the dried yeast and the sugar.

■ Put the aniseed, orange rind and water into a saucepan, bring to the boil and cook for 1 minute. Strain and cool.

■ Rub the butter into the flour mixture then add the beaten egg, and 3 tablespoons of the aniseed liquid. Mix well. Turn the dough on to a floured surface and knead thoroughly for about 10 minutes, then place in a greased bowl and cover with well-greased cling film until doubled in size.

■ Turn the risen dough on to a floured surface and knead for about 2 minutes or until smooth. Divide into eight equal rounded portions to make individual buns. Place six of the portions on a well-greased baking tray, spacing them well apart. The other two portions are for the 'bones' and 'tears'. To shape the bones, divide one portion into two and roll each half between your floured hands, allowing it to hang down so that its own weight makes it stretch, until it is about 1 cm (½ inch) in diameter. Roll the strips gently on a floured surface. Cut each strip into six, so that you have 12 in total. Brush one strip with a little water on one side, and place it across a bun, from one side to another. Repeat with another strip to form a cross on the top of the bun. Flatten on top.

■ Divide the remaining portion of dough into 10. Roll six pieces into balls the size of walnuts. Brush each bun with water in the centre of the cross, and press a walnut-sized ball of dough gently on the top. Then make 24 'tear drops' out of the remaining dough. Wet them and place them at random between the rolled 'bones' (the crosses).

■ Cover with a warm, damp tea-towel and leave in a warm place for about 40 minutes to rise again. Bake in the centre of the oven at 200°C, 400°F, Gas Mark 6 for 10–15 minutes. Lightly beat the egg white and brush it over each bun, then sprinkle with caster sugar and pink sugar crystals (if using). Cool and serve for breakfast, tea or supper.

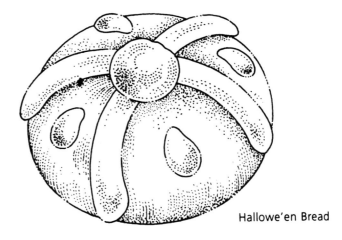

Hallowe'en Bread

Dulce de Calabaza

—————— STEWED PUMPKIN WITH CINNAMON AND ORANGE ——————

SERVES 8

Dulce de Calabaza en Tacha is the right name for this dessert. It originates from Oaxaca where it is cooked with raw cane sugar which turns the dish a muddy black. It has no eye-appeal at all but is full of nutrients. So if you opt for nutrition use muscovado sugar instead of white sugar. Shelled pumpkin seeds can be found at health food shops or Chinese supermarkets.

I often get asked why we use garden lime in this dish. The answer is that it toughens the surface of the pumpkin pieces and in so doing prevents the pumpkin from becoming mushy whilst cooking. It is harmless, 80 million Mexicans eat it daily in their corn *tortillas*, and, what is more, it is a good source of calcium.

With the exception of pumpkin soup, pumpkin is only eaten in Mexico either crystallised or stewed and served as a dessert. This very original dessert tastes delicious served with cream. Don't be put off by any other pumpkin dish you might have disliked before – this is totally different. Preparation should start two days in advance. The dessert freezes well or keeps in the refrigerator for 5 days.

INGREDIENTS

750 g (1½ lb) raw pumpkin	750 g (1½ lb) granulated or muscovado sugar
2 tablespoons garden lime (see page 23)	
2 litres (3½ pints) water	two 10 cm (4 inch) sticks cinnamon
juice and finely chopped rind of 2 oranges	75 g (3 oz) shelled pumpkin seeds

METHOD

■ Cut the pumpkin into 5 cm (2 inch) squares and prick them all around with a fork. In Mexico, the skin is left on and pricked because this helps to keep the flesh together, but you may peel it off if you prefer. In a non-metallic container, dissolve the lime in half the water and soak the pumpkin in this solution overnight.

■ Drain the pumpkin and rinse under running water. Boil the orange rind in the remaining water for about 30 minutes or until soft. Add the pumpkin, orange juice, sugar, cinnamon and shelled pumpkin seeds, and simmer for 10 minutes or until the pumpkin softens. Remove the pumpkin and place it in a heatproof dish. Boil the syrup for another 30 minutes or until reduced by half, then pour immediately over the pumpkin. Cool and serve at room temperature.

Gelatina de Leche

———— MILK JELLY ————

SERVES 6

Jelly is a popular dessert in Mexico. I can remember the jelly vendor carrying his colourful jellies in a glass box and selling them in the streets of Mexico City. The jellies had a base of greaseproof paper and were half milk, half strawberry or lime, with one raisin in the middle. This is an all-milk jelly which is especially popular with children as it tastes like jellied ice cream.

INGREDIENTS

½ can (200 g/7 oz) of sweetened condensed milk	½ teaspoon vanilla essence
2 egg yolks	600 ml (1 pint) cow's milk
2 tablespoons sugar	1½ tablespoons powdered gelatine
	6 crystallised cherries

METHOD

■ Put all the ingredients, except the cherries, in a blender, and blend at top speed for 1 minute. Pour into a saucepan and stir continually over medium heat until the mixture comes almost to the boil. Remove from the heat and pour into a 1.2 litre (2 pint) jelly mould. Cool, then refrigerate for 4 hours or until firmly set. To serve, dip the mould into hot water for a few seconds, invert on to a serving dish and garnish with the cherries.

Ensalada de Frutas Tropicales

——— TROPICAL FRUIT SALAD ———

SERVES 4

Nothing is more refreshing than this salad served well chilled, especially after a meal featuring hot chillies. Basically, any fruit can be used, but the ones chosen for this recipe are the most popular in Mexico.

INGREDIENTS

75 g (3 oz) strawberries, hulled and halved	juice of ¹/₂ lemon
¹/₂ cantaloupe melon, deseeded and cubed	100 g (4 oz) granulated sugar
100 g (4 oz) watermelon, deseeded and cubed	150 ml (¹/₄ pint) water
	2 tablespoons icing sugar, sifted (optional)
1 large banana, peeled and sliced	150 ml (¹/₄ pint) double cream, whipped (optional)
2 oranges, peeled and sliced	
100 g (4 oz) paw-paw, deseeded and cubed	2 tablespoons pecan nuts, to decorate
1 mango, stoned, peeled and cubed	

METHOD

■ Mix all the fruits with the lemon juice in a heatproof bowl. Dissolve the granulated sugar in the water over low heat, then bring to the boil and strain over the fruits. Mix the icing sugar with the cream and whip them until stiff. Refrigerate the fruit salad and the cream separately until cold. Serve the fruit salad with the cream and a sprinkling of pecan nuts.

Crema de Mango

──────────── MANGO CREAM WITH ALMONDS ────────────

SERVES 8

This is my own version of a delicious dessert, suitable for a dinner party. It will keep in the refrigerator for up to 2 days, and it freezes extremely well.

Mangoes are cultivated abundantly in Mexico, having been introduced from the Philippines after the Spanish Conquest. The most popular kinds grown are the Manila which has a pale yellow skin and is very sweet, and the commonly known *Petacón*, a type of Alfhonso mango with a rosy red skin, which is more readily found in Britain. If you can't find fresh mangoes, however, don't hesitate to use canned mango. Alternatively, make this dessert with fresh peaches, strawberries or raspberries instead. Easy and tasty, it's a great success with any of these fruits.

INGREDIENTS

900 g (2 lb) stoned, peeled mango flesh	juice of 1 lemon
400 g (14 oz) can of sweetened condensed milk	2 oranges, peeled, segmented and halved or 200 g (7 oz) can pineapple cubes
600 ml (1 pint) double cream	100 g (4 oz) flaked almonds, to decorate

METHOD

■ Put the mango in a blender, and blend to a purée, then rub through a sieve. Whip the condensed milk and double cream together until light and fluffy, then fold in the lemon juice. Fold in the fruit purée, orange or pineapple pieces and pour the mixture into individual serving dishes. Decorate with the almonds just before serving.

DRINKS

▲▲▲▲▲▲▲▲▲▲▲▲▲▲▲▲▲

MEXICO has such an incredible variety of drinks that there is something for everyone. There are sustaining drinks like *atole* that will more than satisfy early morning hunger pangs, as well as the delightful *chocolate caliente*, (hot chocolate) which might be drunk for breakfast or supper accompanied with a sweet bread roll, or perhaps between meals. *Café de olla* is a strong coffee boiled with cinnamon and muscovado sugar, which is drunk from early morning till nightfall.

For the children there are innumerable colourful and tasty cool drinks made from fresh fruits. They range from the well-known *limonada* (lemonade), to any other kind of fruit 'ade', as well as fresh fruit juices like orange juice, coconut milk and sugar cane juice. *Licuados* are a range of fruit drinks made in an electric blender.

Mexico's most famous alcoholic drink is tequila, both white and golden (aged). White tequila is primarily an aperitif, but hardened drinkers will drink it all night long – neat! The gold *Tequila Añejo* can be offered instead of port, after the meal. *Tequila Rebozado* is the most subtle of all, being aged for longer. For beginners and people like me, there are a variety of fun tequila cocktails which aren't quite so lethal!

Mezcal, like tequila, is made from an agave and is an unrefined spirit. It is often sold with a maggot in the bottle (more for sensationalism than for taste). A more native alcoholic drink is *pulque* (made from another type of agave) which is popular with the working classes but is quickly losing ground to the excellent Mexican beers.

Finally Mexico offers the popular clear and dark rums which are of good quality and, of course, *Kahlua*, a coffee liqueur flavoured with vanilla which has also gained international popularity. Mexican wines, red and white, are now found in most liquor shops in the United States and Europe and are slowly gaining acceptance.

Chocolate Caliente

DRINKING CHOCOLATE

SERVES 4

When Mexicans think of chocolate, we think of the warm, sweet, creamy drink we had for breakfast and supper as children. Not that we don't also enjoy chocolate sweets as they are sold in Europe today, but traditionally we *drink* our chocolate, just as the pre-Columbian Indian emperors drank theirs. The best drinking chocolate has good froth on it (similar to a *cappuccino* coffee) and to get good results we usually have in the kitchen a special jug with a high neck. The chocolate is poured into it and then whipped with a *molinillo*, a sort of egg whisk made from one piece of wood out of which several rings have been carved. By rolling the *molinillo* between the palms of the hands very fast, a thick foam starts to form on the top of the drink. (This can also be achieved with an electric hand mixer.) We drink chocolate hot or cold and usually we serve sweet buns with it. Chocolate comes in different flavours, vanilla, cinnamon or plain, but I prefer to mix the flavours as I prepare my chocolate.

INGREDIENTS

200 g (7 oz) plain chocolate	¼ teaspoon vanilla essence
900 ml (1½ pints) hot milk	sugar to taste
¼ teaspoon ground cinnamon	

METHOD

■ To melt the chocolate, break the bar into small pieces and place them in the top of a double saucepan or in a heatproof bowl over a saucepan of simmering water. Stir the chocolate with a wooden spoon to speed the melting process and avoid sticking or burning. Add the hot milk slowly, stirring all the time until well mixed. Add the cinnamon and vanilla.

■ Place the saucepan directly on the heat (or transfer the chocolate from the bowl to a saucepan) and bring to the boil. Lower the heat and whisk briskly with an egg beater, a balloon whisk or an electric mixer for 1–2 minutes. Remove from the heat and carry on whisking until bubbles form high over the mixture. Serve hot in individual cups, making sure to divide the foam equally. Add sugar to taste.

VARIATION

For cold chocolate, cool the mixture after it boils, refrigerate and serve. It will not froth when cold.

Atole

MAIZE DRINK

SERVES 4

Atole is an excellent winter drink. Mild-flavoured, thick and served piping hot, it takes the place of porridge for breakfast. It is often flavoured with fresh fruit purée, such as strawberries, mango, pineapple or raspberries. When it is flavoured with dark chocolate it is called *champurrado*.

INGREDIENTS

50 g (2 oz) *masa harina* (see page 19)	225 g (8 oz) fresh fruit purée or 100 g (4 oz) plain cooking chocolate, grated
600 ml (1 pint) water	
1 litre (1³/₄ pints) milk	pinch of ground cinnamon
175 g (6 oz) caster sugar	

METHOD

■ Dissolve the *masa harina* in the water. Bring the milk to the boil and pour the dissolved *masa harina* into it, stirring constantly. Simmer for 3 minutes. Mix in the sugar and fruit purée or chocolate. Serve in individual mugs, garnished with cinnamon.

Café de Olla

COFFEE WITH CINNAMON AND BROWN SUGAR

SERVES 4

Café de Olla, also known as Mexican Coffee, is simply delicious. It is considered the drink of the masses as it probably originated due to a lack of quality coffee. Coffee was introduced into Mexico by Spain and into Spain during the Arab occupation. It grows extremely well in Mexico and excellent coffee is drunk in most Mexican homes and restaurants. Basically, adding muscovado sugar and cinnamon to the coffee makes it more like a liqueur and I find it is a good palate-cleanser. However, because so many people prefer to avoid sugar, I make the syrup which I offer separately to those who wish to try this spicy coffee. It tastes best served from a pottery mug. It is an ideal way of freshening up leftover coffee.

INGREDIENTS

5 tablespoons water	4 mugs hot coffee
4 tablespoons muscovado sugar	
13 cm (5 inch) stick cinnamon or 1 teaspoon ground cinnamon	

METHOD

■ Heat the water, sugar and cinnamon, stirring until the sugar is dissolved. Boil for 3 minutes, then strain into a jug, to serve as an alternative to cream with freshly brewed coffee. If leftover coffee is used, put all the ingredients, including the coffee, in a saucepan, bring to the boil, stirring continually, and simmer for 2–3 minutes. Serve immediately.

Limonada

FRESH LEMONADE

SERVES 6;
makes about
1 litre (1³/₄ pints)

Fruit-flavoured cool drinks are always on offer in Mexico. In the streets they are called *agua fresca*, often sold from ten-gallon glass barrels that appeal to the eye. They are easy to re-create at home. Plain iced water is hardly ever offered at the Mexican table; for this reason this recipe is a family favourite. This is very quick to make and it keeps for days refrigerated uncovered. Limes, which in Mexico are squeezed to make *limonada*, are not suitable for this recipe.

INGREDIENTS

1 lemon, quartered	6 tablespoons brown or granulated sugar
1 litre (1³/₄ pints) cold water	

METHOD

■ Place the lemon quarters, skin and all, in a blender. Add 300 ml (¹/₂ pint) of the cold water and the sugar. Blend at top speed for 45 seconds only, then strain into a jug. Pour the rest of the water through the lemon peel in the strainer to wash out any remaining flavour and natural oils. Discard the lemon. Refrigerate the lemonade; serve with ice cubes.

Agua de Jamaica

SORREL FLOWER WATER

SERVES 8

Agua de Jamaica is a tea made with a wild dark red blossom called *Flor de Jamaica*. It is rich in vitamin C and not the same as the wild sorrel known in England. Fresh sorrel blossoms are traditionally used around Christmas time; it grows wild in the Caribbean region and it is so popular in Mexico that it is enjoyed the whole year round. Dried flowers are bought in the markets and they are so flavourful that they are used to make delicious jam or even an inventive sauce to serve with lamb instead of mint sauce. In England fresh sorrel blossoms are occasionally found at West Indian shops during the Christmas season. Prepared with a little ginger, it makes a colourful drink. If you use fresh flowers, you need to double the quantity of sorrel. Preparation starts 4 hours ahead of time.

INGREDIENTS

100 g (4 oz) dried *Flor de Jamaica* (sorrel flowers)	100 g (4 oz) caster sugar
2.7 litres (4½ pints) water	

METHOD

■ Wash the flowers in a sieve under cold running water. Place them in a saucepan with half the water and simmer for 5 minutes. Cool and strain into a jug. Put the sugar in a saucepan with 8 tablespoons of the remaining water and simmer for 3 minutes or until the sugar has dissolved. Add it to the jug. Add the remaining water and chill until required.

Tequila con Limon

TEQUILA WITH LIME

SERVES 4

Tequila is the most popular alcoholic drink in Mexico and is served as an aperitif. Well-hardened drinkers can drink a bottle in one night, but one or two drinks are quite sufficient for anyone I know! Traditionally, tequila is served at room temperature with lime quarters and coarse salt. The idea is that you put a pinch of salt in the hollow at the base of your bent thumb on the top of your hand. You then hit the stretched-out fingers of the hand with the salt on it and the salt jumps into your open mouth (this needs practice). Otherwise, lick the patch of salt, then swallow a shot of tequila in one go, and finally suck the lime. You can actually feel the tequila glowing as it goes down your throat, all the way to your tummy!

INGREDIENTS

1 tablespoon coarse salt	100 ml (4 fl oz) tequila
1 lime, quartered	

METHOD

■ Serve the salt and the lime on a plate. Pour the tequila into four glasses and instruct your guests on what to do.

Cocktail De Tequila

TEQUILA SUNRISE

SERVES 4

This popular cocktail is a beautiful colour and reminiscent of Mexican sunrises. It can be made with almost any fruit juice, plus a touch of grenadine syrup.

INGREDIENTS

250 ml (9 fl oz) tequila (white or gold)	8 ice cubes
350 ml (12 fl oz) tablespoons unsweetened orange or pineapple juice	4 tablespoons grenadine syrup
4 teaspoons egg white, lightly whipped	4 pieces fresh fruit, to garnish

METHOD

■ Mix the tequila, fruit juice and egg white in a blender at high speed for 20 seconds. Divide the ice cubes between four tall glasses and pour in the tequila mixture. Tilting each glass as you do so, spoon in the grenadine and drop a piece of fruit into the drink. The flavour of the egg does not come through but produces a lovely bubbly drink.

Cocktail Margarita

TEQUILA AND LIME JUICE COCKTAIL

SERVES 4

If you make freshly squeezed lime *margaritas*, you will make a name for yourself. There is no substitute for the aromatic fresh lime and, believe me, the satisfaction of making the most delicious margarita in town is enough reward for the hard work of squeezing the limes!

If you are having a party and you need several margaritas, squeeze all the limes together, mix with the measured tequila and Triple Sec or Cointreau, and refrigerate. Prepare the rims of the glasses as instructed and have them ready to pour the margarita mixture over the crushed ice as your guests arrive.

INGREDIENTS

2 large limes	4 tablespoons Triple Sec or Cointreau
table salt	8 ice cubes
225 ml (8 fl oz) tequila	

METHOD

■ Squeeze the juice from the limes, reserving the lime halves. Moisten the rims of four cocktail glasses by rubbing with the reserved squeezed lime halves. Put the salt on a saucer and dip the rim of the glasses in it. (Do not attempt to do this with water as it dissolves the salt.)

■ Place the lime juice in a blender, add the tequila, the Triple Sec or Cointreau and the ice cubes, and blend at high speed for 30 seconds. Pour into the chilled glasses. If you wish to make this drink weaker, add more ice and less of the mixture to each glass.

Tequila Slammer

MAKES 1 drink

I have not seen this drunk in Mexico and I can only imagine that it is because of the Mexican's familiarity with tequila – they have learnt to respect its strength! However, my son Richard assures me that it was a best-seller at his 'Tacos and Tequila' stall and indeed I had occasion to verify it when I assisted him at an Oxford Summer Ball. It is definitely not my style of drink as it goes to the head extremely quickly. This, I am told, is because the alcohol in the tequila starts breaking up before it is ingested and is therefore absorbed more readily into the bloodstream. Richard describes it as 'playing Russian roulette with a sub-machine gun'!

INGREDIENTS

25 ml (1 fl oz) tequila

25 ml (1 fl oz) champagne (lemonade can be used as substitute)

METHOD

■ Pour the tequila into a 'shot' glass and pour champagne over it. Cover the top of the glass firmly with the palm of your hand. Lift the glass with the other hand and slam the glass on to a firm table. If the glass hits the table with sufficient vigour the mixture will become very bubbly and turn white. It should be swallowed in one gulp. The effect is lethal!

Ponche De Tequila

TEQUILA PUNCH

SERVES 20

One good way of getting the party going once and for all! This punch is so good, my guests are happy to drink it all through the night which is ideal for big parties.

INGREDIENTS

750 ml (1¼ pints) tequila (white or golden)	two 500 ml (18 fl oz) bottles American ginger ale
225 g (8 oz) caster sugar	500 ml (18 fl oz) soda water
600 ml (1 pint) fresh orange or pineapple juice	500 ml (18 fl oz) tonic water
juice of 6 limes	40 ice cubes
dash of Angostura bitters	

METHOD

■ Mix the tequila, sugar, orange juice, lime juice and Angostura bitters together and refrigerate. Just before serving, mix in the ginger ale, soda and tonic waters. Place two ice cubes in each glass before pouring in the punch.

Rompope

TEQUILA EGG-NOG

MAKES about
750 ml (1¼ pints)

Rompope is a well-liked drink in Mexico, most popular amongst children and old ladies. This is an advocaat type of drink, a glorified 'egg-nog' prepared in the old days by the nuns in the convents and sold to help sustain their heavy expenses. It is generally offered before the meal as an aperitif instead of *jerez* (sherry), although it is quite sweet.

INGREDIENTS

400 g (14 oz) can of sweetened condensed milk	½ teaspoon vanilla essence
300 ml (½ pint) milk, chilled	3 tablespoons ground almonds (optional)
4 egg yolks	150 ml (¼ pint) tequila, rum or vodka

METHOD

■ Place all the ingredients in a blender and mix at top speed for 45 seconds. Strain into chilled glasses. This drink will keep in the refrigerator for up to 4 days.

Licuados

BLENDED FRUIT DRINKS

MAKES about 300 ml ($^{1}/_{2}$ pint)

Licuados are drinks made from fresh fruits, blended in an electric blender with either milk or water. The choice of fruits that can be used is mind-boggling. *Licuados* take the place of orange juice for breakfast, or a mid-morning coffee break. Of course, when you are walking along the streets of Mexico under the blazing sun and you come by a *licuado* stall, you are compelled to stop and have a cool drink. Here are some ideas.

INGREDIENTS

LECHE Y PLATANO (MILK AND BANANA DRINK)

1 banana

250 ml (9 fl oz) cold milk

2 teaspoons sugar

pinch of ground cinnamon

NUEZ (MILK AND NUTS)

50 g (2 oz) pecan nuts, walnuts, almonds or hazelnuts

250 ml (9 fl oz) milk

1 teaspoon sugar

FRESAS (STRAWBERRY AND ORANGE JUICE)

225 g (8 oz) strawberries

150 ml ($^{1}/_{4}$ pint) fresh orange juice

2 tablespoons sugar

METHOD

■ Blend the ingredients for each drink for 30 seconds at top speed and serve with ice cubes in tall glasses. Drink straight away.

Te de Yerbabuena

MINT TEA

SERVES 2

Yerbabuena (good herb) is the name given to garden mint because it is believed it will cure almost any digestive malady. Mexico City is 7,000 feet above sea level and, due to this, strong drinks go to your head very quickly and your digestion becomes sluggish. Having a cure-all tea to offer after the meal is ideal. This is a mild tea, which I prefer to conventional tea; it can be served hot or cold.

INGREDIENTS

10 leaves garden mint	sugar, to taste
350 ml (12 fl oz) water	

METHOD

■ Boil the mint in the water for about 5 minutes, strain into tea cups and drink very hot, sweetened to taste. For a cool drink, strain, allow to cool and garnish with fresh mint leaves.

Cerveza Michelin

LIME AND BEER ON ICE

SERVES 1

This is a novel idea which I came across for the first time a few months ago when I visited Valle de Bravo, near Mexico City. I am not a keen alcohol drinker so I keep away from it in favour of fresh fruit juices, but I have to say this has got to be the most refreshing drink I have ever had.

INGREDIENTS

4 ice cubes	a shake of salt
¹/₂ lime	1 bottle of Mexican beer, well chilled

METHOD

■ Place the ice cubes in a glass, squeeze the lime juice on to them, add a shake of salt, then pour the cold beer into the glass.

INDEX